# More Praise for A *Full-H*

"Jake Owensby is the real deal, a brilliant theologian, yet also a deeply human person amongst us. His life and work are about love and freedom, the joy and fulfillment of service, a life devoted to the common good, and the individual's richest possible heart-filled awakened spiritual life. I love his work."
—Anne Lamott, New York Times bestselling author of several books, most recently *Somehow: Thoughts on Love*

"Jake Owensby shows how the Way of Love as taught by Jesus of Nazareth is the way forward through life's uncertainties and challenges to a truly full—and full-hearted—life."
—The Rt. Rev. Michael Bruce Curry, 27th Presiding Bishop and Primate of The Episcopal Church and author of *Love is the Way*

"Bishop Jake writes in a spirit of friendship, as if we were all sitting at his dinner table. As a master teacher, he makes the connection between our lives and the God revealed to us in Jesus. If you want to know what it looks and feels like to be a Christian, read this book. If, as a Christian, you could use a little encouragement, look no further."
—The Rt. Rev. Mariann Edgar Budde, Bishop of the Episcopal Diocese of Washington DC, author of *How We Learn to Be Brave: Decisive Moments in Life and Faith*

"*A Full-Hearted Life* is Jake Owensby at his brightest and most heartening. As always, Jake delights and informs, but most of all, during this often-discouraging time, he encourages. Believers are sure to find encouragement to be better Christians in this time and place. Would-be believers will find new rationale for faith. And if you are a preacher like me, you'll find lots of sermons, too!"
—Will Willimon, Professor of the Practice of Christian Ministry, Duke Divinity School; United Methodist Bishop, retired; and author of *Changing My Mind: The Neglected Virtue for Faithful Ministry*

"In this winsome and accessible book, Jake Owensby reminds us that when we follow Jesus authentically and courageously, we can create profound change in ourselves, our families, and our communities. This quietly powerful volume is an invaluable guide for Christians struggling to withstand the seismic changes in the church and the world that are facing us all."

—The Most Rev. Sean W. Rowe, 28th Presiding Bishop and Primate of The Episcopal Church

"You have in this book an instruction manual, a guidebook, a road map for keeping and finding and renewing the heart. When I finished reading this, during a difficult time in our world, there was more of me than when I began. I had not lost heart. And I give thanks to Jake for that."

—The Rt. Rev. Brian Cole, Bishop of the Episcopal Diocese of East Tennessee

"We live in an anxious, angry age, longing for meaning but overwhelmed by myriad possible meanings and haunted by the suspicion that there might not be any meaning at all. With gentle wit and wisdom, Owensby invites us to consider following Jesus into the heart of God where we can find rest, purpose, and the full-hearted life for which we long."

—The Rt. Rev. Matthew Gunter, Bishop of Wisconsin

"The future of Christianity hinges on it being a life to be lived more than doctrines to be affirmed. Bishop Owensby understands this and writes not only to help us understand it too, but also to inspire us to be about the task of vocational discipleship—full-hearted devotion to Christ in our particular arenas of everyday living."

—Dr. Steve Harper, retired professor of Spiritual Formation; author; and elder in The United Methodist Church

"Countless times, I have asked earnest and faithful persons about to be baptized or confirmed, 'How will what you are about to do this Sunday morning affect how you will greet Monday?' More times than not I get a deer-caught-in-the-headlights look and stunned silence. Now comes *A Full-Hearted Life* to answer the deep crisis of discipleship in our churches! This is a real help for pastors and people seeking God's purpose in these real times."

—The Rt. Rev. A. Robert Hirschfeld, Bishop of the Episcopal Diocese of New Hampshire, and author of *With Sighs Too Deep for Words: Grace and Depression*

"As pastor of a forward-facing church in times of 'dark-glass faith,' I am keenly aware of our need for voices to lead the way. Jake Owensby is an engaging guide for deeper faith-seekers. *A Full-Hearted Life* invites us into the real-life questions we find ourselves asking and brings clarity to the challenges of a faith-thirsty world."

—Rachel Billups, senior pastor, New Albany United Methodist Church, New Albany, OH

"*A Full-Hearted Life* is a book for any Christian who wonders and worries about the competing truth claims in our post-Christian world, and for nonbelievers too, who will meet a disciple of Jesus who looks for the best in others, delights in a deep conversation, and is willing to be changed by learning from the wisdom of all those he encounters on the way. A beautiful, inspiring, and encouraging book!"

—The Rt. Rev. Scott Barker, Bishop of the Episcopal Church of Nebraska

"Our secular age doesn't oppose religion so much as marginalize it. Thus, Christians must know why they follow Jesus and how their discipleship leads to a full-hearted life. Jake Owensby addresses the most practical faith questions while drawing from a vast array of rich spiritual resources that will bless and inspire readers."

—Lovett H. Weems, Jr., distinguished professor of church leadership emeritus, Wesley Theological Seminary, Washington, DC

"In a world of fragile beliefs and competing truths, Jake Owensby's *A Full-Hearted Life* stands as a beacon of hope, clarity, and beauty.

This isn't just another book about faith—it's a roadmap to discovering how Christian belief can infuse every aspect of our lives with meaning and purpose. Owensby's warm, pastoral voice makes even the most complex ideas feel like a heart-to-heart conversation. Whether you're a seasoned believer or a curious skeptic, this book will challenge and inspire you to live more fully."
—Cameron Merrill, United Methodist pastor and editor of MinistryMatters.com

"Jake Owensby has provided a reflection on how to live as followers of Jesus in a world desperately in need of hearts filled with love and curiosity, as forces of grace and goodness in this life."
—The Rt. Rev. C. Andrew Doyle, Bishop of the Diocese of Texas and author of *Citizen: Faithful Discipleship in a Partisan World*

"A *Full-Hearted Life* is a book for us all at a time when love seems to be in short supply. A master of integration, Jake Owensby seamlessly blends the pastoral and theological, and demonstrates the essential connection between belief and practice. While reading this book, my inner voice kept saying, 'This is the life for which everyone yearns.' If you want to expand your vision of life and really learn what it means to flourish, this book is for you."
—Rev. Dr. Paul W. Chilcote, research fellow of Wesley House, Cambridge; award-winning author of several books, including *The Fullest Possible Love: Living in Harmony with God and Neighbor*

Jake Owensby

# A Full-Hearted Life

Following Jesus
in This Secular Age

Nashville

A FULL-HEARTED LIFE:
FOLLOWING JESUS IN THIS SECULAR AGE

*Copyright © 2024 by Abingdon Press*

ISBN: 9781791035037

Library of Congress Control Number: 2024947623

MANUFACTURED IN THE UNITED STATES OF AMERICA

*In gratitude for teachers who changed my life,*
*especially Charlene, Tom, Kent, and Bernadette*

# Contents

*The heart has its reasons which reason knows nothing of. . . .*
*We know the truth not only by the reason, but by the heart.*

—Blaise Pascal, *Pensées*

*A new heart I will give you, and a new spirit I will put within you,*
*and I will remove from your body the heart of stone and give you*
*a heart of flesh. I will put my spirit within you.*

—Ezekiel 36:26-27a

*Our lives and humanity are untidy: disorganized and careworn. Life on earth*
*is often a raunchy and violent experience. It can be agony just to get through*
*the day. And yet, I do believe there is ultimately meaning in the chaos,*
*and also in the doldrums.*

—Anne Lamott, Stitches: A Handbook
on Meaning, Hope and Repair

*Practical theology is the need to interpret the 'where' of Jesus Christ in our experiences of the now.*

—Andrew Root, *Christopraxis: A Practical Theology of the Cross*

Prologue

# Searching for a Full-Hearted Life

IT WAS THE FALL SEMESTER of my junior year in college. The term was winding down. Completing one big assignment stood between me and a much-needed Christmas break. I was writing a long research paper about Immanuel Kant's theory of beauty. It was complicated stuff and painfully slow going. Midnight came and went on the term's final Saturday. With one more edit I would be able to call it quits. But my brain had ground to a halt. Those last revisions would have to wait until morning. Well, until first light at least.

I had been working in the living room. My apartment mates had called it a night hours ago. So I flipped on our ancient black-and-white TV, lowered the volume to a whisper, and turned out the lights. Ted Turner's pre-cable superstation was running an *It's a Wonderful Life* marathon. I had come into that familiar Christmas story just as the main character, George Bailey (famously played by Jimmy Stewart), faced financial ruin, sank into despair, and attempted suicide. Heaven sent a bumbling, kindly angel named Clarence to rescue George and to show him that the world would not have been the same without him. As the credits rolled, I turned the volume all the way down and sat in silence by the silver glow of the television. It seemed to me that George had utterly lost heart. That's what despair is, after all. The rock bottom of being disheartened. And I recognized that, while I wasn't in despair, I was growing disheartened. What Anne Lamott says about her friend Tim sounds very much like where I found myself that night:

> [Tim] craved a reset, freedom from the same ten worries and concerns, freedom from the same ten things he was mad about, freedom from the obsession with the bathroom scale. Freedom from the perfectionism, the disappointment in himself, the dissatisfaction that has run like an underground river through him for a lifetime. Freedom from dragging this all along with him everywhere like a dinosaur's tail. He longed to feel more peaceful, more present and alive.[1]

The imminent crash of his savings and loan business had brought on George's crisis. What the philosopher Charles Taylor calls the fragilization of belief was the source of my own heart trouble.[2] Let me explain.

We all want to lead a full-hearted life. To have a sense of who we are, that we are being true to ourselves, and that what we do in this world matters. To be passionate about a purpose, to have genuine relationships with others, and to take joy in being alive. Our ideal of a full-hearted life emerges from our foundational beliefs, from our worldview. These beliefs provide for us answers to life's big existential questions. Who am I? What is my purpose? How does my life fit into the larger scheme of things? Does the path I'm on really lead me to a full-hearted life? What is that life anyway? When our beliefs become fragile, our answers to life's big questions grow unreliable and the point of life can feel uncertain. Being disheartened

---

1. Anne Lamott, *Somehow: Thoughts on Love* (New York: Riverhead Books, 2024), 28.
2. Charles Taylor, *A Secular Age* (Cambridge, MA: Harvard University Press, 2007), 303–4.

is the emotional expression of this existential instability. When our beliefs no longer reliably help us make sense of our circumstances, we grow disheartened and may fall into despair. A broad range of observers agree that our culture exhibits the classic symptoms of a crisis of despair: anxiety, addiction, and aggression.[3] A basic premise of this book is that a pervasive fragilization of belief lies at the root of our crisis.

I will say more about fragilization in a moment. But first it's important to stress that the fragilization of belief has nothing to do with an individual's spiritual or moral failings. Instead, the fragilization of belief is a defining mark of our secular age. How I'm using the term "secular" here may initially be confusing to some of you. After all, many people use the word *secular* as practically synonymous with "anti-religious" or "unbelief." And while there is a rise in the number of people who do not affiliate with any organized religion, everyone has to ask life's big questions. Even people who reject every hint of the supernatural and insist that nothing exists apart from matter will have to sort out how to be find meaning for themselves. To put this another way, the defining mark of our secular age is not the absence of belief, but rather the effect on our consciousness of the sheer number of competing belief systems. That effect is fragilization. We are inundated by information from the internet and bombarded by competing truth claims in the media. Moreover, we are aware like never before of the faith traditions and the belief systems that find our own Christian beliefs untenable, strange, or even ridiculous. Most of us know (or at least know of) Jews, atheists, Muslims, Buddhists, agnostics, and spiritual-but-not-religious individuals. Their commitment to a belief system that differs from our own indicates that Christianity can be put into question. Actually, it tells us that our beliefs are in fact questioned by others on a regular basis. It follows that we don't have to believe what we believe. We could believe something else entirely. Moreover, we are very

---

3. Alex Pattakos and Elaine Dundon, *Prisoner of Thoughts: Viktor Frankl's Principles for Discovering Meaning in Life and Work* (Oakland, CA: Berrett-Koehler Publishers, 2017), 54.

likely to have internalized, perhaps unwittingly, beliefs from our surrounding culture that we have misidentified as or have mistakenly assumed to be expressions of the gospel. The result can be either confusion or internal conflict, neither of which will reliably support our sense of life's purpose, value, and meaning.

Whether we like it or not, we dwell within this secular age. So even when we believe in Jesus profoundly (as I do), our belief is still fragilized. We cannot simply forget that we have options. Instead, to experience the full-hearted life we seek, we must clearly articulate for ourselves and for others how our belief in him answers life's big questions for us and thus infuses our life with meaning. And that is the project of this book. My aim is to show how believing in Jesus gives us a sense of who we are, why we're here, what the full-hearted life is, and how to move toward that life. So, this is not a work of traditional apologetics. I'm not setting out to offer logical proofs that God exists or that Jesus is God incarnate or that all those alternative belief systems are false. Put simply, the aim of this book is to help you see for yourself and to explain to others how Christian belief and Christian practice help you lead a full-hearted life.

# Note to the Reader

AT THE END OF EACH CHAPTER, you'll find a set of questions. These are meant to prompt your own reflection as an individual, and discussion, if you read the book in a group. We hope the questions also help you to draw your own conclusions about belief, meaning, and the full-hearted life you wish to lead.

Following the questions, a brief prayer is provided. This is for readers who are Christian or those who wish to try this means of connection with God.

# PART I

# BELIEF, TRUST, AND CONVERSION

*On any given morning, I might not be able to list for you the facts I know about God. But I can tell you what I wish to commit myself to, what I want for the foundation of my life, how I want to see. When I stand with the faithful . . . and declare that we believe in one God . . . I am saying, Let this be my scaffolding. Let this be the place I work, struggle, play, rest. I commit myself to this.*

—Lauren Winner,
*Still*

Chapter One

# Everybody Believes Something

ELLEN ASKED, "YOU'RE A CHRISTIAN, right?"

"Sure. Why do you ask?"

"Professor B. said that Christians are cannibals. At Communion you eat the body and blood of Jesus. Eating human flesh makes you a cannibal. Are you really a cannibal?"

She was being serious. I was a philosophy professor at a secular university. Ellen was one of a group of students who regularly showed up during my office hours to argue with me about life's big questions. Who am I? Is there really a God? How do you know the difference between good and evil? Does my life have a purpose? These are not idle questions. How we answer them forms the foundation of the full-hearted life we all seek. I had taught them the basic skills of critical thinking and the value of clear-eyed reasoning. Many of my students knew vaguely that I was a Christian, but we didn't discuss my personal beliefs in class. They rightly assumed that I meant what I said about the importance of rationally examining our own beliefs and values. So Ellen was understandably stunned and disappointed to hear that I indulged in some sort of primitive, superstitious ritual. That's why she made an appointment outside my regularly scheduled office hours to demand an explanation from me. How could somebody so educated and so committed to critical thinking indulge in such a repulsive practice? Eating human flesh, even symbolically, is uncivilized and just gross. It made no sense to her.

Professor B. taught creative writing. Like me, he encouraged his students to wrestle with life's big questions for themselves. Everybody needs meaning in life to flourish. We all need to know why we're doing what we're doing. And the answers to these questions provide the pillars of a full-hearted life. They are the "why" that keeps us going. My colleague's assumption was that his students had passively received answers to these questions from their pastors, parents, and Sunday school teachers. To make these religious answers their own or to shed them in favor of others, students must first examine their tacit beliefs. Notice that B.'s assumption was that religion was the usual source of his student's default belief systems. Ellen had grown up in an entirely nonreligious family. She had never been to a worship service and knew only the most superficial things about Christian beliefs and practices. Her beliefs—the beliefs that led her to question my integrity—had come from nonreligious sources. At the time I had no way of knowing that Ellen was giving me a preview of our current spiritual landscape. Everybody believes something, but religion no longer plays a dominant role in shaping those beliefs. Many people have no religious background. And even those sitting in our pews on Sunday have frequently drawn their answers to life's big questions from sources other than religion. Influencers on TikTok, X (formerly Twitter), and Instagram probably shape the spiritual consciousness of at least as many people as even the most effective preachers.

To put this another way, plenty of Christians have internalized secular answers to life's big questions as if those answers were genuinely Christian. And so in order to be authentic disciples in our current context, we Christians need to honestly examine why we do what we do. That's what this book is all about. We'll be looking at what Jesus has to say about life's big questions and explaining how his answers provide life-sustaining, life-transforming meaning. But I'm getting ahead of myself. Let's step back and look more intentionally at the changing place of religion in our social and cultural landscape.

## A Changed Religious Landscape

All around the country you can see community centers, apartment buildings, restaurants, and derelict buildings that used to be houses of worship. The authors of *Beyond Doubt: The Secularization of Society* tell us that up to ten thousand churches close each year in the United States.[4] As a bishop I've participated in the sad process of shuttering a few myself. In the book I just mentioned, authors Kasselstrand, Zuckerman, and Cragun offer this as evidence that the secularization hypothesis is true. In short, that hypothesis is that religion will decline as modern society progresses. People will increasingly rely upon science, the social sciences, and logic to guide their personal, social, and political lives. To put this another way, rational processes will steadily take the place of adherence to religious teachings and dogmas for our decision-making. Correlatively, worship and church membership will become increasingly irrelevant to most people.

Whether or not you agree that secularism is destined to make institutional religion an artifact of a bygone age, you might at least agree that we are living in an era of dechurching. Pews are getting emptier, and membership rolls thinner. Compare for instance the religious landscape of the 1950s to today's. Seventy years ago, the percentage of people reporting no religious affiliation at all (the Nones) hovered between zero and 2 percent. Today the

---

4. Isabella Kasselstrand, Phil Zuckerman, and Ryan T. Cragun, *Beyond Doubt: The Secularization of Society* (New York: New York University Press, 2023), 21.

Nones account for anywhere from 20 percent to 30 percent of the American population.[5] To be clear, there's plenty of spiritual longing and curiosity among the Nones. Only a small percentage of them are atheists. And even a percentage of those atheists believe in a higher power of some kind, just not the biblical God.[6] But they are not finding the sense of connection, the guidance, and the sustenance they seek within institutional religion.

In their book *Secular Surge*, David Campbell, Geoffrey Layman, and John Green argue that when it comes to belief, Americans fall into one of four groups.[7] There are religionists, non-religionists, secularists, and religious secularists. For her series on the decline of religion for *The New York Times*, commentator Jessica Grose interviewed Campbell by phone and asked him to say more about these groups. Here's how she described his response:

> He told me he thinks of religionists, intuitively, as people who are "highly religious and don't have much secularism in their lives." Non-religionists aren't affirmatively secular, they just don't have much of a religious worldview. "They haven't really thought about truth, meaning, etc.," he said. Secularists "have determined that they find truth in philosophy and science and sources like that, and not from religious texts." And religious secularists "see the world through a secular lens, but they also have a foot in a

5. See Frank Newport, "Slowdown in the Number of Religious Nones," Gallup, December 9, 2022, https://news.gallup.com/opinion/polling-matters/406544/slowdown-rise-religious-nones.aspx; and also Gregory A. Smith, "About Three-in-Ten U.S. Adults Are Now Religiously Unaffiliated," December 14, 2021, https://www.pewresearch.org/religion/2021/12/14/about-three-in-ten-u-s-adults-are-now-religiously-unaffiliated/.

6. Michael Lipka, Patricia Tevington, and Kelsey Jo Starr, "8 Facts About Atheists," https://www.pewresearch.org/fact-tank/2019/12/06/10-facts-about-atheists/, Pew Research Center, February 7, 2024.

7. David Campbell, Geoffrey Layman, and John Green, *Secular Surge: A New Fault Line in American Politics* (Cambridge: Cambridge University Press, 2021).

religious community." They have "found a way to accommodate both ways of seeing the world."[8]

And that brings us back to Ellen and the problem of making sense of the Christian faith in our present context. I assured her that we are not cannibals and briefly explained that a sacrament is a visible sign of God's invisible grace. That didn't initially get through, so I shifted gears. She could think of grace as God's love for us. Communion is a spiritual meal on analogy with the physical experience of eating supper. Our bodies need nourishment to survive. Our souls need nourishment to thrive. Grits are the body's food. Love is food for the soul. What I said wouldn't go very far with seminary professors. Maybe you're rolling your eyes a bit too. But please keep in mind that I was looking for a way to connect with a very bright, well-read young woman who had no acquaintance with Christian doctrine or practice. After I finished my explanation, Ellen nodded her head and sat silently for a bit. Eventually she said, "Thanks, Doc," and left. I was glad to see her at the next office hour.

Here's what that long ago conversation with Ellen taught me about the secular age we inhabit. Even though attachment to organized religion is in decline, ours is not an era of unbelief. On the contrary, everybody yearns for a full-hearted life and believes something about how to lead such a life. Ellen is a good example. She was raised in a thoroughly nonreligious home. She had no experience of traditional spiritual beliefs or practices. However, it would be imprecise to characterize her as an unbeliever. On the contrary, she had a belief system that simply didn't include God. You may consider what I'm about to say a contradiction in terms, but I think it's accurate to say that Ellen had a nonreligious faith. I have in mind here William James's definition of faith: "Were one asked to characterize the life of [faith] in the broadest and most general terms possible, one might say that it consists of the belief that there is an

---

8. Jessica Grose, "Why Do People Lose Their Religion? More Than 7000 Readers Shared Their Stories," https://www.nytimes.com /2023/06/07/opinion/religion-nones.html.

unseen order, and our supreme good lies in harmoniously adjusting ourselves thereto."[9] She was deeply offended by the prospect that I was a cannibal, even in a symbolic sense. Merely pretending to eat human flesh violated her deeply felt convictions. Moreover, she judged that I might be a hypocrite. What I had said in class and how I acted outside of class seemed to contradict each other. And in her mind hypocrisy counted as a serious moral transgression. All of this points to deeply held convictions about the worth of human beings and the nature of good and evil. She may not have belonged to an organized religious tradition, but Ellen held some foundational beliefs that shaped her moral judgments and guided her actions. That's a form of faith. And everybody has one. To live in a secular age is to be surrounded by a sea of alternative faiths. So one of the primary challenges of following Jesus in a secular age is to explain how a full-hearted life in this world is anchored in a relationship with him. This world requires of us a reason why we walk the Way of Jesus rather than one of the many available alternatives. After all, there are genuinely admirable examples of humanity whose belief systems have not the first thing to do with the crucified and risen Jesus. To give that reason, we'll first take a closer look at the idea of faith.

## What Is Faith?

Ellen had also studied with another friend of mine, a fellow philosopher who taught ethics. Professor S. had been trained as a rabbi, so her knowledge of the Hebrew Scriptures was extensive. And she was no stranger to the New Testament. But she no longer believed in the God described in those texts. I admired her moral integrity, her generosity, her persistent kindness, and her dogged commitment to justice. And even though she found no reason to believe in anything supernatural, she genuinely respected the

9. William James, *The Varieties of Religious Experience. A Study in Human Nature* (Oxford: Oxford University Press, 2012), 46.

world's religious traditions and my own personal faith. From time to time, we shared lively, good-natured conversations about God's existence. S. never budged from her brand of atheism. And yet, it would be incorrect to say that she had no faith. On the contrary, atheism was her faith. She had converted to it from Judaism after serious, prolonged reflection. A good God, she reasoned, would not allow the relentless, horrific suffering that we frequently see in this world.

As I mentioned above, organized religion—especially Christianity—occupies a different place in our culture now than it once did for earlier generations. Worship attendance has declined. It is still declining. Fewer people identify with organized religion now than ever before. And crucially, belief in God is seen widely as a choice made for personal reasons, not as a response to a church's teaching authority. Religious diversity is a clear fact of our culture. All of us see loads of nice, normal people pursuing happy, productive, and virtuous lives based on beliefs that contrast with and perhaps even contradict our own. Those who decry the rise of secularism as the rejection of faith may be missing the point. It's just one more faith. Ours is not a faithless age. It is an age of many faiths.

Faith—whether you are a Christian or a Jew, a Muslim or a Buddhist, an atheist or an agnostic—is more than a set of concepts to which we give an intellectual nod. It is a paradigm or a worldview through which we understand who we are and by which we navigate our world. Every choice we make and each of our actions embodies our faith. We draw our identity, our purpose, our sense of personal significance, our understanding of good and evil, justice and injustice from our view of how the world works and how we fit into it. In 2005 the late writer and professor David Foster Wallace illustrated what I'm saying about faith with the following parable:

> There are these two young fish swimming along, and they happen to meet an older fish swimming the other way, who nods at them and says, "Morning, boys. How's the water?" And the two young

fish swim on for a bit, and then eventually one of them looks over at the other and goes, "What the hell is water?"[10]

In Wallace's parable, water represents what philosophers call "tacit beliefs." They are our preconscious assumptions. Philosophers have argued that, whenever we focus on any object of thought or on any perception, we draw on previously accepted beliefs, values, and past experiences to make sense of the new idea or sensation. Think of tacit beliefs like glasses that you have to wear in order to see things clearly at all. You see *through* those glasses. You don't look *at* them. They make it possible for you to see other people, plants, animals, and words on a printed page. I'm using the word *faith* to refer to our *foundational* tacit beliefs. It's how we make sense of our lives from the simplest daily routines to the choices we make at decisive turning points.

Clearly, some tacit beliefs are not foundational. For instance, if I were to change my opinion about which toothpaste is best or about which actor had played James Bond most convincingly, it would have a negligible effect on the meaning of my life. These are trivial matters. We can change our minds about such things without turning our whole world upside down. We're not basing our lives on them. But Jesus is clear that we have to build our lives on *something*. And the choice we make about our foundation is crucial. Foundational beliefs have existential consequences. We build our lives on them. Jesus put it this way:

> "Everyone, then, who hears these words of mine and acts on them will be like a wise man who built his house on rock. The rain fell, the floods came, and the winds blew and beat on that house, but it did not fall, because it had been founded on rock. And everyone who hears these words of mine and does not act on them will be

10. Cited in Jenna Krajeski, "This Is Water," *The New Yorker*, September 19, 2008, https://www.newyorker.com/books/page-turner /this-is-water.

like a foolish man who built his house on sand. The rain fell, and the floods came, and the winds blew and beat against that house, and it fell—and great was its fall!" (Matthew 7:24-27)

Everyone has a faith. A foundational set of tacit beliefs. This is no less true for committed atheists than it is for Christians and Jews and every other religious tradition. We can't avoid using tacit beliefs. That's how the human mind works. Conversion from one faith to another doesn't just subtract out this, that, or the other discrete idea and replace it with a more adequate one. Faith is a web of concepts and practices. They are all interconnected, hanging together and supporting one another. If you pull at one strand, the rest are affected. Conversion to a new faith transforms who we are in the very marrow of our being. Cephas becomes Peter. Saul becomes Paul. "So if anyone is in Christ, there is a new creation: everything old has passed away; look, new things have come into being!!" (2 Corinthians 5:17). And as we will discuss in the next chapter, conversion is not only a movement from one faith to another. Conversion is also the process of going ever-deeper into the faith that already defines us. And that is why I find Wallace's advice so helpful for following Jesus in a secular age.

Wallace urges us to examine our tacit beliefs. Especially our foundational beliefs. Instead of passively receiving them from the church hierarchy, from our parents, from our teachers, and from our peers, we can and should make our beliefs our own—and take greater responsibility for what we are doing and leaving undone on this planet—by reflecting on them critically. We should ask ourselves, "Why do I believe these things?" For some of my fellow Christians, this may sound suspiciously like doubt, and they see doubt as the enemy of faith. But other Christian thinkers like Peter Enns and Brian McLaren explain that this sort of doubt comes with recognizing that our understanding of spiritual things is always partial.[11] As Paul wrote, "For now we see only a reflection, as in a mirror, but then we will see face to face. Now I know only in part; then I will know fully, even as I have been fully known" (1 Corinthians 13:12). With experience and prayer, with study and service, our perspective broadens over time. We won't get the whole picture in this life, but our horizons broaden. It's like what Sarah Bessey says: "Anyone who gets to the end of their life with the exact same beliefs and opinions as they had at the beginning is doing it wrong."[12] Asking this question at ever-deeper levels of commitment to Christ—why do I believe these things?—is the process of lifelong conversion in which all discipleship is rooted. I'm going to turn to a more detailed discussion of conversion in the next chapter. But first, let's look at how the reason for adopting Christian beliefs and following Christian practices rests on our search for the full-hearted life.

## The Will to Believe

One of the marks of contemporary life is that any belief we hold is challenged, if only implicitly, by the fact that other individuals and other groups find what we believe implausible or already believe something else wholeheartedly. Any faith we claim as our own appears to be one option among many. We are compelled to offer a reason for adhering to one belief system rather than another. In our current social and cultural context, the advice offered in 1 Peter resonates as perhaps never before: "Always be ready to make your defense to anyone who demands from you an account of the hope that is in you" (1 Peter 3:15).

---

11.   See Peter Enns, *The Sin of Certainty: Why God Desires Our Trust More Than Our "Correct" Beliefs* (San Francisco: HarperOne, 2016); and Brian McLaren, *Faith After Doubt: Why Your Beliefs Stopped Working and What to Do About It* (New York: St. Martin's Essentials, 2021).

12.   Sarah Bessey, *Out of Sorts: Making Peace with an Evolving Faith* (New York: Howard Books, 2015), 88.

Many of my fellow Christians will point to their Bibles as evidence for God's existence and the truth of the Resurrection. It's the Word of God, after all. And let me be clear, I too believe that it is God's word. But think about it. You have to already believe in God to think of the Bible as the Word of that God. The pages of Holy Scripture draw me closer to the divine, shape my actions, challenge my assumptions, and change my perspective about other people because I already believe that I meet Jesus there. My belief is the lens I need in order to read in the first place. Without belief, the important stuff of the Bible—the life-shaping, life-transforming stuff—would never come into clear focus for me.

Another set of Christians insist that true faith is based on no evidence at all. Belief requires taking an irrational leap of faith. But I resist the idea that faith is a form of irrationality. I'm confident that God gave us a mind so that we would use it. After all, great Christian theologians and philosophers down through the centuries have offered proofs for the existence of God. Thinkers like Augustine, Anselm, Thomas Aquinas, Renè Descartes, and much more recently John Polkinghorne have argued logically that there must be a God. Back in my philosophy-professor days, I taught many of these arguments. Some are more forceful than others. All have met with strong and reasonable criticism. None will convince everybody. And besides, even if these proofs were perfectly valid, they would only demonstrate that there is some divine being or other. This is a long way from providing a reason to believe in something like the resurrection of Jesus. Adopting these more specific beliefs would require what we will call a pragmatic reason. That is, we can look at the existential consequences of applying such a belief to our daily life. Does acting on such a belief make life more meaningful, add value, give us a sense of purpose? In other words, does acting on such a belief lead to the full-hearted life we seek? If it does, then believing in God or the Incarnation or the resurrection makes pragmatic or existential sense.

This way of approaching beliefs comes from the philosophical movement called Pragmatism. Thinkers like John Dewey and

William James argued that an idea's validity is tied to its real-world, practical consequences. The truth and meaning of a belief are bound up with what happens when we act on it. An agnostic might argue that, before acting on a belief about something like the resurrection, we should still wait for some solid evidence that acting this way will result in the kind of life for myself and for the world that we want to have. Does it really solve the existential problems of meaning and value and purpose with which we are struggling? The pragmatist philosopher William James responds that, in most cases, remaining agnostic is the prudent approach to take. However, in a narrow set of cases, we do not have the luxury of assuming a wait and see posture. We simply have to act even when there is no logical or scientific basis upon which to assert a belief. Crucially, from the perspective of Pragmatism, every action we take embodies a belief. To act is to believe. And belief in God is a prime example of such a narrow case. Every action embodies a belief in God or a rejection of that belief.

To be more precise, belief in God is one of those relatively rare cases that James called a genuine option.[13] For an option to be genuine in James's sense, it must meet three criteria. It must be living, forced, and momentous. Let's take these criteria one at a time. An option is *living* if we're considering only hypotheses that we would genuinely consider acting upon. For instance, I really might eat a hamburger for lunch, accept an invitation to give the keynote address at a conference, or spend the day with my grandchildren. By contrast, a dead hypothesis is one I would never even consider putting into action. You won't catch me seriously flapping my arms to fly to work or looking up at the sky to spot a flying pig. If James found himself talking to someone for whom the whole God thing is unthinkable, he wouldn't bother to make his case. This argument

---

13. William James, "The Will to Believe." See a free version at https://courses.lumenlearning.com/suny-classicreadings/chapter/william -james-on-the-will-to-believe/, though a scholarly version is included in *The Will to Believe and Other Essays in Popular Philosophy* (Cambridge: Cambridge University Press, 2014).

is meant only for those who would genuinely consider acting on a belief in God.

With a *forced* option we are facing an either/or. There are two and only two possible hypotheses. You must choose. There's no avoiding it. So when it comes to belief in God, there are only two hypotheses: act on belief in God or do not act on it. Agnostics will insist that there is a third option: suspend belief. Don't choose. Just opt for "maybe" and get on with your life. But James's point is precisely that life goes on. At each instant you will act. Refusing to act is itself an action. And every action expresses a belief. Remember, James is a pragmatist. To believe is to act. So agnostics may claim to withhold judgment about God, but everything they do expresses either belief in God or disbelief. Failing to act is to disbelieve.

Finally, the option must be *momentous*, not trivial. The stakes must be high, and the choice cannot be undone. For instance, imagine that your life's ambition is to be an astronaut. You have been given the chance to be the first person on Mars. There's only ever going to be one first person on Mars. If you refuse to go on that mission to Mars, you will forever lose the chance to be the first person to walk on the Martian surface. By contrast, if I pass up dessert after dinner, I could grab a piece of pie later in the evening. It's no big deal. When it comes to believing in or rejecting belief in God, our individual lives and the fate of our world are at stake. We become who we are through our actions, and the consequences of our choices leave a mark on our world. Each moment of our lives confronts us with a choice: act on a belief in God or on the belief that there is no God. To put this another way, with every action we turn toward or away from the full-hearted life envisioned by Jesus. In the following pages I will say more about what such a self and such a world look like and why we should move toward them. But for now, the point is that Christian faith is making a choice to turn toward Jesus. To entrust our lives to him. And this is a process—a process of conversion that unfolds one day at a time for our whole lives.

## Spiritual Reflections and Exercises

1. Talk about your own spiritual/religious journey. Did you grow up in a faith tradition? Attend worship? How was that experience for you then? How do you look at it now? If you did not grow up in a faith tradition, what is your perception of faith traditions like Christianity? What interests, attracts, or repels you about faith?

2. Have your beliefs about yourself, the world, and God changed over time? Talk about some beliefs that you have left behind. Some that have evolved. Have any remained the same? What are they? Where are you now on your spiritual journey? What do you believe? Doubt? Hope? Where do you get meaning and a sense of purpose?

3. Is there anything that has challenged your faith or your rejection of faith? Have you thought about giving faith a try or another try or walking away from it? How about changing your denomination? Your congregation? Leaving church? Tell a story about that. Why and where have you found yourself now?

4. Talk about what has reinforced your beliefs.

5. Have you ever had conversations with people whose beliefs are very different from your own? What did you learn from them? What did you find attractive, threatening, strange, or unsettling? Was this conversation hard for you? Energizing? Frustrating?

6. Take a look at your regular routines and habitual choices over the past month. Pretend that you are an alien from a different planet looking at you as a stranger. Answer these questions on the basis of what you observe: Where do you find meaning? What are your highest values? What is your purpose in life? (It's cheating to say what's going on in your

own head. Act as if you can only see what that alien could see about that stranger from a distance.)

*Prayer:* Holy and merciful God, help me to be honest with myself about the beliefs that guide my life. Forgive me when I rest upon anything less than you. And help me to entrust my life entirely to your infinite mercy. In Jesus's name. Amen.

*What needs to be changed in us? Anything that makes us
the sole center of ourselves. Anything that deludes us into thinking
that we are not simply a work in progress, all of those degrees, status,
achievements, and power are no substitute for the wisdom that a
world full of God everywhere, in everyone, has to teach us.*

—Joan Chittister,
*Illuminated Life*

Chapter Two

# Lifelong Conversion

MY FRIEND R. AND I DECIDED to do some winter camping in the Smoky Mountains. A couple of days after Christmas, we loaded his old Ford Fairlane with our backpacks and headed north from Atlanta. The dawn greeted us as R. steered the car through a series of tight turns. The trees parted to my right, revealing a steep drop into the valley far below. I only noticed the absence of a guardrail when I heard R. shout, "Whoa!" He had hit a patch of ice. The car slid out of control and began heading sideways over the cliff. My life flashed before my eyes. Or more accurately, my pounding heart made an essential truth about my life inescapably clear. My existence had always been hanging by a thread. And so it is with all of us. We are fleeting, fragile, vulnerable creatures.

Philosophers and theologians call our kind of existence "contingent being." To put it simply, our existence at each instant depends upon something—upon Someone—beyond us. We did not bring ourselves into being. We cannot ensure that we will be alive in the next second. For the most part, this sort of thought remains an abstraction for us. However, when life flies apart at the seams, when our life circumstances overwhelm us, or when we face our own death, we can have an existential aha moment. We experience in a visceral way the powerlessness of our own wit, know-how, and willpower. They cannot prevent the bottom from falling out from under our lives. And this insight can be an occasion for conversion. To be clear, I don't have in mind here a change in our beliefs, like moving from doubting God's existence to asserting God's existence. Rather, an aha moment like this shifts our spiritual focus. Previously we may have wrestled intellectually with the abstract idea of God, whether or not some being like that exists somewhere. Now we struggle to entrust our lives to a power greater than ourselves. To seek God's guidance, to pursue God's purposes, to see my neighbor as God's beloved when I can't see that for myself. And that struggle is a lifelong process.

## Conversion Is a Process

The New Testament contains a number of accounts of conversion experiences. Paul's encounter with the risen Jesus on the road to Damascus may be the most familiar (Acts 9:1-19). This persecutor of the fledgling Christian community becomes the Apostle to the Gentiles after meeting Christ. Then there's Philip and the Ethiopian eunuch (Acts 8:28-40). On the road from Jerusalem to Gaza, Philip came across a member of the Ethiopian queen's court. The Ethiopian had traveled to Jerusalem to worship. Philip found him struggling with a passage from Isaiah: "Like a sheep he was led to the slaughter" (Acts 8:32b). Hearing Philip explain that the passage was about Jesus, the Ethiopian asked to be baptized. Both of these stories feature non-Christians changing course and following Jesus. The story of Peter walking on water may not have made your list of familiar conversion stories (Matthew 14:22-33). However, it's important because it illustrates that conversion is the pattern that defines a full-hearted life. You see, Peter was already following Jesus. And the story shows us that a full-hearted life is about going deeper and deeper in our relationship with Jesus. As you may recall,

Peter, along with the other disciples, was battling a storm at sea when Jesus came strolling across the waves. They were all shocked and more than a little frightened. And yet, Peter stepped out of the boat to join his rabbi. Peter realized that walking on water was not in his skill set. Stepping out of the boat was a choice—with his very life—to trust Jesus enough to follow him wherever he led. Even crazy, risky, unsafe places—places like reconciling bitter relationships, forgiving the unrepentant, and loving determined enemies. OK, so Peter sank. Jesus had to pull him to safety. This trust thing takes some growing into. It's a lifelong process. And that brings us back to the Smokies in December.

The right side of the car slid off the road onto the shoulder. Rain and snow had thoroughly saturated the mud along the shoulder, so the passenger-side tires plowed a deep rut that brought the car to a halt. We both exited on the driver's side. Given what I said above about Peter, you've probably already guessed that I'm not telling you my one-time conversion story. Instead, this is just one of many turning points, large and small, in a lifelong conversion narrative. I'll be spending the rest of my life, and maybe all of eternity, learning to entrust my life to God. To put that a different way, conversion takes a lifetime. One day at a time.

In the Anglican tradition, the tradition to which I belong, we don't deny that many people have remarkable, life-changing moments marking a new relationship with the risen Christ. However, our thinking about conversion is influenced by the Benedictine approach to spiritual formation. One of the vows taken by the monks is *conversatio morum*. You'll often see that phrase translated as "fidelity." What it means is a promise to pursue a daily pattern of living that leads us closer and closer to God. That is to say, Benedictine monks make a commitment to lifelong conversion. So it might be helpful to say that the Christian life is rooted in conversion rather than saying that it *begins* with conversion. The word *begin* may suggest to you a moment when a switch has been forever flipped. Instead, I urge you to think of conversion as an intention with which we enter each new day. That's not to say that we make no progress in the spiritual life. On the contrary, our relationship

with the risen Christ deepens. We can grow in wisdom and virtue. Nevertheless, every day presents us with situations in which we
must live out our commitment to Christ in three ways.[14] We promise (1) to renounce evil, (2) to turn to Jesus as Savior and to trust in
his grace, and (3) to follow and obey him as Lord.[15] Let's examine
each of these commitments in turn.


## Renouncing Evil

We *renounce* the spiritual forces that rebel against God, the evil
powers of this world, and our sinful desires. The ways of this world
can be cruel and dehumanizing. And from time to time, we feel compelled to act on our self-centered thoughts and impulses. Becoming
a follower of Jesus does not insulate us from the world's destructive
energies or exempt us from experiencing selfish impulses. Instead,
we commit ourselves to a lifelong pattern of resisting those unholy,
dehumanizing forces and choosing to participate with God's grace.
In other words, renunciation is not one and done. It's the ongoing,
day-by-day work of living in a fractured world that God is actively
mending.

One of my colleagues is an old-school illustrator. And what he
told me about his craft helped me see how renunciation is our commitment to cooperate with God's redemption of a creation marred
by selfishness and violence. Today's animators use software to create
computer-generated images. With the click of a button, they can
delete an image and start all over. By contrast, the artists in the

---

14. Like me, you might find the image of the labyrinth to be a helpful illustration here. Found in many churches, a labyrinth is a winding,
circular path that leads to a center point. There are no dead ends. No
choices to make about which path to take. There is just the one. But some
stretches along the path turn temporarily away from the center. Others
turn back toward it. Importantly, each step brings you closer to your destination even when it seems to be doing exactly the opposite.

15. I have drawn this pattern from the Baptismal Rite found in the
1979 Book of Common Prayer (New York: Church Publishing Incorporated), 299–311.

early days of the Walt Disney Studios drew each frame by hand. It was painstaking work. When you're using pen and ink, you're committed at the very moment that the pen touches paper. You've made a mark that you can't erase. Initially I thought that this resulted in lots of discarded paper. After all, nobody's perfect. Everybody makes mistakes. But I was wrong. At least my colleague didn't go about his craft that way. He said that he would incorporate every stroke of the pen, even the errant ones, into the final picture. He doesn't discard a flawed image and start all over. He takes what he's got right in front of him—smudges, crooked lines, and all—and crafts something lovely from it. This is how God relates to the creation. And as we commit ourselves to the lifelong process of renouncing the powers that disfigure the creation, we grow in our cooperation with God's grace, in being God's agents of healing and transformation.

John the Baptist taught in fiery terms that God will clean up this messy world of ours by punishing wrongdoers and rewarding the righteous. God will separate the wheat from the chaff. The wheat will be gathered in. The chaff will be burned. At least, that's how he thought about justice and God's judgment at the height of his preaching ministry. He understood himself as preparing the way for the Messiah. And indeed, he was. Except he may not have been so clear about what the Messiah would get up to. When the Baptist actually saw the Messiah in action with his own two eyes, it made him wonder—wonder about the nature of divine justice; about the way that justice and love fit together in the one God.

After Herod had tossed him into the royal dungeon, John wrestled with who his cousin Jesus actually was: "Is he the one? Is he the Messiah? But he doesn't act like a messiah. Or else, maybe I need to rethink what the Messiah will be like. Maybe I need to rethink what God is like." So John sends his disciples to ask Jesus straight up, "Are you the one who is to come, or are we to expect someone else?" (Luke 7:20b). Jesus came to show us who God really is. That's why he said this to John's disciples:

> Go and tell John what you have seen and heard: the blind receive their sight, the lame walk; those with a skin disease are cleansed;

the deaf hear; the dead are raised; the poor have good news brought to them. And blessed is anyone who takes no offense at me. (Luke 7:22-23)

In Jesus God embraces the disfigured world we actually inhabit and makes it lovely again by the power of love. Divine justice is the creative power of love. Justice is not merely retribution. It's perfect restoration. God recognizes that life gets messy. And God responds to that mess by showing up with the love that created the entire cosmos, that brought the Israelites home from Babylonian captivity, and that raised Jesus from the dead.

The divine love is a force, not just an affection. It's the only power capable of making something good and beautiful and holy from even our most ghastly, chaotic messes. But God doesn't do this in isolation. God works through the likes of you and me. And that means that we have to respond to the love that God is pouring out. To make that love—not our narrow self-interest—our center of gravity. That's what it means for us to renounce. Each day we are drafting what we hope will be a full-hearted life. We have made and will make mistakes. We've inherited or suffered from mistakes made by others. And as it turns out, the picture we are drawing is more than a self-portrait. Whether we realize it or not, we are participants in God's restoration of all things in even our simplest acts of kindness and compassion, acts of forgiveness and patience. God works through us in God's own grand drawing project. In Jesus we see that God does not toss our mistakes into a cosmic waste bin. Instead, God says, "Let's see what we can make of this together. Something new. I think it's going to be beautiful."

## Turning and Trusting

Next, we *turn* to Jesus as our Savior and *trust* in his grace and mercy. You see, we long for our lives to have lasting significance. And yet, as the psalmist says, "[Our] days are like grass; they flourish like a flower of the field; for the wind passes over it, and it is gone, and its place knows it no more" (Psalm 103:15-16). We desire eternity, but our mortal flesh goes down to the grave. Over time, each of us will pass from finite human memory. Our deepest yearning is beyond our grasp. We are powerless to accomplish it. Following Jesus requires an admission of our powerlessness. That admission makes it possible for us to give our lives over to a power beyond ourselves that is greater than ourselves. To trust a Savior whose grace and mercy can do for us what our wit and effort cannot. The psalmist continues, "The steadfast love of the LORD is from everlasting to everlasting" (Psalm 103:17). Admitting our powerlessness is no small thing in this can-do, achievement-oriented world. It takes courage, humility, and wisdom. So when I need a refresher course about my own powerlessness, sometimes I talk to friends who are honestly contending with addiction in one way or another.

A few of those friends are still struggling to stop drinking or using. A larger number are in recovery. Almost all of my friends have a story about an addicted relative, friend, neighbor, or coworker. The pathway to recovery, as well as the key to coping with loved ones in the grip of addiction, begins with learning the crucial lesson that we are powerless. Nobody likes learning that lesson. That's because you really grasp it only when you experience your own powerlessness firsthand. Nobody can do your homework for you. Addicts learn this lesson through misery. They want to stop. They've lost careers, relationships, and health. Their souls are rarely at peace. And yet they are driven by a craving they can neither stem nor control. The friends and families of addicts learn about powerlessness by way of a desperate and broken heart. Neither love nor persuasion nor coercion has had an effect. None of it has moved their loved one toward sobriety. As one friend put it, he discovered that he was just as powerless over his relative's addiction as she was over her desire for the substance of her choice.

Addiction's foundational lesson is also a core lesson for faith. A life of faith is rooted in the acceptance of grace. And grace is a gift for the powerless, not a reward for the spiritually muscular. Jesus teaches this lesson in a myriad of ways. For instance, he once crossed the Sea of Galilee with his friends after a long day of teaching. As evening approached, they had scrambled into a boat and cast off. Jesus had promptly fallen asleep. A windstorm swept across the sea. The boat started taking on water. The disciples feared that they might go under. So they woke Jesus. He promptly silenced the wind and calmed the waves. Only after the storm had passed did Jesus ask them about their faith (Mark 4:35-41). Jesus first let them experience powerlessness. Then he asked them to reflect on their faith. He wasn't interested in giving them a creed or a catechism to memorize. Jesus had come to open their hearts and minds to the God who is always already present.

In the third and fourth centuries, the Desert Mothers and Fathers committed themselves to a life of rigorous asceticism and prayer. They would spend hours in their humble cells wrestling with their own inner demons. Contrary to what you might expect, their aim was not to conquer and eradicate their selfish or violent or lustful impulses. Instead, pushing themselves to their human limit, they would eventually fail to perfect themselves. Those unwelcome thoughts and desires would pass away briefly and then inevitably return. These desert monastics struggled to defeat their own worst angels until those angels showed themselves to be too strong for them. In their failure, they discovered in a profoundly personal way their need for grace. Their need for a love that will always embrace them in their raggedy imperfection. By falling flat on their faces, they experienced being picked up and dusted off by a power greater than themselves. Encountering their own powerlessness up close revealed to them their very personal need for God.[16]

Paul once urged us "not to accept the grace of God in vain" (2 Corinthians 6:1). What I take him to mean is that God's grace transforms us. Paradoxically, acknowledging our powerlessness makes us powerful. Except it's a power that the world knows little about. Accepting grace makes us compassionate. It moves us toward embracing the imperfect people around us, not because we can change them or improve them or get some reward, but because we now know that they are the beloved. Just like us.

---

16. Thomas Merton edited a collection of their sayings in *The Wisdom of the Desert* (New York: New Directions Books, 1960).

## Follow and Obey

Finally, we promise to *follow* and *obey* Jesus as Lord. Jesus summarized the law that we should obey. He told us to love God completely and to love our neighbor even when we may not feel like it. The summary is not hard to remember. But it's difficult to apply to all of life's complexities. Following Jesus means to accept his guidance, to rely upon his support, and to emulate his example. He is our trustworthy guide. But it is still up to us to choose to follow his and only his lead.

After Sunday worship at one of the congregations in my diocese, I met with the church's leadership for the standard review of finances, attendance figures, evangelism strategies, and the like. One of the leaders was visibly angry. He said nothing until we came to the "Other Business" item at the end of the agenda. Referring to my sermon, he said, "Where do you get off telling us to love our enemies? They're our enemies! They're dangerous. We have to defend ourselves." Taken aback, I was at a loss for words. Several seconds passed. The priest of the parish broke the silence by saying, "The bishop was quoting Jesus. Those words are from the Sermon on the Mount. It's in Matthew's Gospel." My critic didn't respond, but he was obviously still fuming and appeared to be unconvinced.

This exchange came to mind later when I listened to an interview with *Christianity Today*'s editor-in-chief Russell Moore. Here's what he said:

> Multiple pastors tell me, essentially, the same story about quoting the Sermon on the Mount, parenthetically, in their preaching—"turn the other cheek"—[and] to have someone come up after to say, "Where did you get those liberal talking points?" And what was alarming to me is that in most of these scenarios, when the pastor would say, "I'm literally quoting Jesus Christ," the response would not be, "I apologize." The response would be, "Yes, but that doesn't work anymore. That's weak." And when we get to the

point where the teachings of Jesus himself are seen as subversive to us, then we're in a crisis.[17]

In other words, Christianity is in crisis because self-identified Christians are using their own political, social, moral, and cultural views to assess the soundness of Jesus's teaching. Strictly speaking, for Christians it should be the other way around. We should test the validity of our thoughts and the trustworthiness of our passions by whether or not they adhere to what Jesus says.

It seems to me that Jesus was getting at something like this when he asked his disciples, "Who do you say that I am?" (Matthew 16:15). He was challenging his followers to examine where he really fit into their lives. Or to put it in terms of the vows of the Baptismal Covenant, did we really mean it when we accepted Jesus as our Lord? As Lord, Jesus is neither a coercive drill sergeant nor a micromanaging boss. He is a wise friend. As we'll discuss in detail in chapter 5, wisdom is the art of navigating life's complexities. Nobody is born wise. And advanced age does not guarantee wisdom. Nevertheless, we acquire wisdom over time if we acquire it at all. Opening our heart, mind, and soul to a person who possesses wisdom is crucial to learning it. We become wise by patterning our lives on how a wise person walks through this world on their ordinary days. How they think, feel, and act in a variety of situations exemplifies a full-hearted life.

The Bible teaches us that the wise don't merely observe the world around them and figure out its patterns all on their own. Instead, they spend a lifetime connecting with the very source of the creation's deep, governing algorithm. Their lives are shaped by the habitual practices of worship, prayer, study, works of mercy, and the pursuit of justice. These practices open us to God's presence in our everyday lives. Jesus is wisdom incarnate. Accepting Jesus as our Lord means that we turn to him to teach us how to

---

17. Scott Detrow, Gabriel J. Sanchez, Sarah Handel, "He Was a Top Church Official Who Criticized Trump. He Says Christianity Is in Crisis," NPR, August 8, 2023, https://www.npr.org/2023/08/08/1192663920/southern-baptist-convention-donald-trump-christianity.

navigate our often messy, confusing lives. As Proverbs instructs, we don't get this life right by relying on our own cleverness and wit. We need a mentor (Proverbs 3:5-6). In other words, Jesus shows us how to live. What he teaches us in the Sermon on the Mount and in his many parables and by his personal example may upend some of our fiercely held assumptions or rein in some of our strong impulses. But when we recognize that we need a mentor to lead a full-hearted life—to live into being the image of God we were created to be—we're admitting that there's much that we do not know and more than a few things that we've gotten wrong along the way. God knows that we're a work in progress. That's why repentance is one of Christianity's traditional practices. We need to admit that to ourselves over and over. Not to get God off our backs. But to accept the helping hand we're always mercifully offered.

## Emotional Motion Sickness

Following Jesus does not deliver us from the struggles of life. My friends, my colleagues, and many of my readers have told me about their burdens and cares and uncertainties. And yet what so many of their stories have in common is a sense that it can be hard, I mean really hard, to be a person. I get it. Me too. We have to navigate grief, conflict, anxiety, disappointment, and frustration. To borrow a phrase from the singer-songwriter Phoebe Bridgers, we all experience emotional motion sickness. She was referring to her emotional state following the demise of a tumultuous, abusive relationship. But I have in mind a sense of spiritual vertigo and emotional nausea. Sometimes, we could really use a break. As Bridgers puts it, "I have emotional motion sickness / Somebody roll the windows down."[18]

Our experience of emotional motion sickness reveals two crucial things to us about us. These things are true every day of our

---

18. Phoebe Bridgers, "Motion Sickness," by Phoebe Bridgers and Marshall Vore, on her album *Stranger in the Alps*, Dead Oceans, 2017.

lives. But mostly we'll only recognize them when life gets so challenging that we can't fly by automatic pilot. We're forced to listen to what life is trying to tell us. Well, actually, to what God is trying to tell us. The first thing is this: Living a full-hearted life is neither simple nor automatic. In fact, we really can't pull it off on our own. We need—we yearn for—a savior, someone beyond ourselves to roll the windows down. Second, the savior we long for is more than someone who only guarantees entrance into the Good Place once our heart stops beating. Instead, we want a Savior who also brings good news to the bad news that we're struggling with right now. As it turns out, that is just the kind of Savior we Christians see in Jesus. He tells us as much in his first hometown sermon after emerging from forty days wandering in the wilderness. In the synagogue he reads the following portion of the Isaiah scroll:

> "The Spirit of the Lord is upon me, because he has anointed me to bring good news to the poor. He has sent me to proclaim release to the captives and recovery of sight to the blind, to set free those who are oppressed, to proclaim the year of the Lord's favor." (Luke 4:18-19; from Isaiah 61:1-2)

Jesus embraces our real, frequently messy lives. Just as they are. He comes to respond to both unjust systems and to the imbalances of our individual lives. Life circumstances can hem us in, isolate us, and leave us wondering just what the point of it all is. Making ends meet, resisting racism, navigating grief, pushing against sexism, contending with toxic relationships, and just trying to understand ourselves and one another is a lot. Sometimes it's just too much. It gives us emotional motion sickness.

Jesus comes to roll the windows down. He does not do this by waving a magic wand and making it all go away. Still less does he guarantee us a smooth ride from now on if we'll just believe in him. Instead, he comes to ride along with us wherever we go. No matter what. As the widely loved psalm reads, "Yea, though I walk through the valley of the shadow of death, I will fear no evil: for thou art with me" (Psalm 23:4 KJV). Our lives are fleeting and oh so fragile.

We are always walking in the valley of the shadow of death. And Christ is already near. Already walking that harrowing way right next to us. As we engage his loving initiative over time through prayer, works of mercy, and study, we find that our spiritual vertigo and emotional nausea can begin to fade. On our best days, they'll give way to tranquility, compassion, courage, joy, and perseverance. This is what lifelong, day-by-day conversion looks like. Conversion to the full-hearted life centered on the risen Jesus. We'll have bouts of emotional motion sickness from time to time. But we trust that there's someone who will roll the windows down. In the next chapters, we will look more closely at this someone, at the Christian concepts of God and the person of Jesus.

## Spiritual Reflections and Exercises

1. As you look back on your life, what turning points do you see? In retrospect, did they affect your thoughts and feelings about God? How do you think about these turning points now? Talk or write about the experience.

2. Have you ever needed a new start? Do you need one now? What helped you or would help you begin again?

3. Have you ever admitted that you were wrong about something you did or failed to do? What led you to that admission? How did you feel before and after? Do you feel as if you grew from the experience? Is there anything you regret right now?

4. How do you respond to Jesus's words about loving your enemy and turning the other cheek?

5. Faith is about trust. Has Jesus shown himself trustworthy to you in your life? How so? If he has not, what would be a sign of his trustworthiness to you?

6. Sometimes following Jesus comes at a cost. What might it cost you? Have you ever experienced the cost of discipleship? What would make the cost worth it to you?

*Prayer*: Holy and merciful God, you have called us to put our trust in your Son Jesus. Give me the courage, the wisdom, and the humility to put my life in his hands in things big and small; and grant me the assurance that nothing I do can turn your love away from me. In Jesus's name. Amen.

# PART II

# HOW OUR BELIEFS SHAPE OUR LIVES

*Here is your life. You might never have been, but you are,*
*because the party wouldn't have been complete without you.*

—Frederick Buechner,
*Wishful Thinking*

Chapter Three

# Made by Love for Love

A CALL CAME INTO THE HOSPITAL'S chaplaincy office from Labor and Delivery. It was at around two o'clock in the morning. A woman had given birth twenty weeks into her pregnancy. Human lungs cannot sustain life at that stage of development. The Hindu parents were grieving the loss of a child. They had requested a minister, and I was the only chaplain on duty. We frequently served people from a wide range of religious traditions or with no faith at all. Our practice was to meet people on their own terms spiritually. Interfaith and non-faith relationships were a routine part of our daily lives in that setting. The hospital protocol required that I check in at the nurse's station. Someone there would brief me about the situation and then provide the room number.

When I arrived, only one nurse was at the desk. She looked up from a chart and then scrupulously ignored me. After a few long seconds it dawned on me that she had no intention of engaging with me. So I said, "Hi! I'm the chaplain on call."

"What are you doing here?"

"Um, well, one of you called me. There's been a death."

"We don't need you. It's just a mass of tissue."

Two other nurses showed up during this exchange. I noticed that they were on the permanent staff and that the nurse with whom I was talking was an agency nurse on temporary duty. The staff nurses were keeping their heads low. I said, "I understand that this is your perspective. But this woman and her husband see things a different way. My role on this team is to meet them wherever they are spiritually. They're having a rough time with this experience. I'm here in response to their call and to see how I can help them." She snapped, "That's ridiculous. It's *just* a mass of tissue."

Finally, I suggested, "Perhaps we should call the supervisor to help us clarify hospital procedure." One of the staff nurses quickly grabbed the phone. In minutes the supervisor arrived, outlined the hospital protocol, and instructed the agency nurse to give me the information I needed. In the room I met a young couple in mourning. They just needed somebody to talk to. So I sat and listened for a while. Eventually, they said that they wanted to see their daughter. Following hospital procedure, I went to the morgue, gently dressed the tiny body in donated, handmade clothing, and brought her back to her parents. They held her for a while, cried some more, kissed her on the forehead, and said goodbye.

Later that night, I spent some time mulling over the phrase "mass of tissue." The agency nurse seemed to have been inviting me to an argument about abortion and when human life begins. But her words actually took me in a different direction. I thought, "What if that is all that any of us are in the end? Just a mass of tissue." One strain of thought in our secular age is what philosophers call materialism. The natural world is all that exists, and that world consists entirely of matter. That is to say, the universe is a mass of tissue. Any talk about supernatural things—and God in particular—is nonsense. By contrast, Christians believe that the material universe has a spiritual origin. God created and continues to sustain all things. In what follows, I'll be contrasting the existential consequences of believing in materialism and believing in a divine Creator. Here's the question: which worldview provides us the most workable framework for living a full-hearted life? And we'll begin where the Bible teaches us to begin. We'll spend time reflecting on our own mortality.

## *Remember That You Are Dust*

The psalmist wrote, "So teach us to count our days that we may gain a wise heart" (Psalm 90:12). Similarly, the author of Ecclesiastes counseled, "It is better to go to the house of mourning than to go to the house of feasting, for this is the end of everyone, and the living will lay it to heart" (Ecclesiastes 7:2). Facing the inevitability of death is also woven into traditional Christian liturgical practice. During the Ash Wednesday worship service, a minister may impose ashes on your forehead with these words: "Remember that you are dust and to dust you shall return." The point of focusing on our finitude is to underscore that we are radically dependent upon God. That life has any meaning at all derives ultimately from God.

Clearly, not everyone believes that the lesson to be drawn from our mortality has the first thing to do with God's existence, much less a divine source of the natural world. As I've said, some secularists argue that this world is all that exists. From a materialist standpoint, you are most certainly dust, metaphorically speaking. And it's best to remember that that's all you are. Only dust. There are no supernatural beings. No God. No soul. Just material stuff. A mature and sober mind accepts the inevitable existential consequences of this view. Death is the end. Period. Intellectually honest people accept this reality. It's just fear of death that drives some people, like Christians, to believe in God. As the late writer and atheist Christopher Hitchens once quipped in an interview, "As long as people are afraid of death and as long as it is suggested that there is a way around that I think religion will stay in the ring. . . . It is based on wishful thinking."[19]

Hitchens was a confirmed and consistent materialist. He believed that we are dust and nothing more. There is no supernatural dimension to reality. Death obliterates each of us. He maintained

---

19. Ed Stoddard, "Author Christopher Hitchens Targets God and Faith," Reuters (June 18, 2007), https://www.reuters.com/article/us -religion-hitchens/author-christopher-hitchens-targets-god-and-faith-id USN0726901520070618.

that religion and its yearning for an afterlife "comes from the bawl-
ing and fearful infancy of our species, and is a babyish attempt to
meet our inescapable demand . . . for comfort, reassurance and other
infantile needs."[20] Still, he wants to insist that death does not rob
our lives of meaning. We can and do make meaning in "friendship, love, irony, humor, parenthood, literature, and music, and the
chance to take part in battles for the liberation of others" without
any reference to God.[21] Even as he endured the agony and indignities of Stage IV esophageal cancer, Hitchens remained true to his
materialist view of existence. He wrote, "It's no fun to appreciate to
the full the truth of the materialist proposition that I don't have a
body, I am a body."[22]

The key here for our purposes is that materialists believe that
they must *make* meaning. They do not *find* meaning in the world
beyond their own hearts and minds. What is real can be verifi-
ably observed, weighed, and measured. There is no such thing as
value, meaning, or purpose out there in the real world. That stuff
is only in your head. It's subjective. Bluntly put, nothing is truly
significant in and of itself. If something or someone is meaningful, it or they are so only to you. Or not. Nothing has inherent
meaning or value. And in the final analysis, that goes for each
and every one of us too. From a consistently materialist point of
view, no person's life has an inherent, enduring significance. The
philosopher Thomas Nagel describes the existential consequences
of materialism this way:

> Even if you produce a great work of literature which continues to
> be read thousands of years from now, eventually the solar system
> will cool or the universe will wind down and collapse and all trace
> of your effort will vanish. . . . The problem is that although there

20. Christopher Hitchens, *God Is Not Great: How Religion Poisons Everything* (New York: Twelve Books, 2007), 108.

21. Christopher Hitchens, *Hitch 22: A Memoir* (New York: Twelve Books, 2010), loc. 5728, Kindle.

22. Christopher Hitchens, *Mortality* (New York: Twelve Books, 2012), 86.

are justifications for most things big and small that we do within life, none of these explanations explain the point of your life as a whole. . . . It wouldn't matter if you had never existed. And after you have gone out of existence, it won't matter that you did exist.[23]

Let me sum up the materialist view of life's meaning like this. You and I are going to die. Our brief span of life may matter immensely to us personally. If we're lucky, while we're still above the dirt, there will be people we care about, and those people will cherish us too. After we die, relatives, friends, and a variety of people whose lives we influenced in some positive way may remember us with great fondness and admiration. In a few cases, our names will endure through our accomplishments: books, monuments, empires, world-shaping feats. And yet, given the length and scope of cosmic history, none of us will be remembered at all. As the commenter Casey K. wrote in response to a *New York Times* article:

How significant are you? How many names of the billions of people that have [walked] on this earth can you recall and with any details of [their] lives? Do you think you will fare any better? . . . Nothing of who you are and what you will do in the short time you are here will matter. . . . So celebrate life in every moment, admire its wonders, love without reservation, and accept its inevitable end.[24]

Casey K.'s prescription for a meaningful life is to celebrate, admire, and love. It's sound advice. But a materialist view of the world does not justify it. After all, there is nothing inherently worth celebrating, admiring, or loving in a thoroughly material world. You can weigh and measure material things to your heart's content, but

23. Thomas Nagel, *What Does It All Mean? A Very Short Introduction to Philosophy* (Oxford: Oxford University Press, 1987), 96.

24. Casey K.'s comment on Tony Schwartz, "The Enduring Hunt for Personal Value," *The New York Times*, May 1, 2015, https://www.nytimes.com/2015/05/02/business/dealbook/the-enduring-hunt-for-personal-value.html.

you will not squeeze out an ounce of value or carry away an inch of meaning from them. For a materialist, value and meaning boil down to how each individual happens to perceive or to feel about things. To be consistent, Casey K. can report that he celebrates, admires, and loves various things and that this makes him feel better about his inevitable descent into the world's compost heap. Additionally, he can point out that many people agree with him. But this agreement among people is a coincidence, not a shared response based on a reality that transcends them all. He has no basis in what he takes to be reality for urging anybody else to do the same thing. To put it simply, if his view of reality is true, he doesn't really find or uncover meaning. He makes it up. Meaning for a consistent materialist is a fiction that dies with its author. By contrast, if we perceive this universe as created by God, we are able to discover meaning in a source beyond ourselves. A meaning that we share with a community over time. We are not just dust. We are created dust. And that makes a profound difference in how we understand life's meaning.

## Created Dust

When I was a philosophy professor, my intro classes always featured a section on proofs for the existence of God. Among them were five from the medieval saint, philosopher, and theologian Thomas Aquinas (1225–74). His starting point for each of these proofs was the natural world as we observe it through the five senses (Summa Theologica, Article 3). His aim was to show that the very essence of the material world—all the dust in the cosmos—points back to a Creator. If you understand dust properly, you have to admit that it was created by something other than itself. To get a taste of his reasoning, I'll outline just one of those arguments: the argument from contingent being. Thomas recognized that every single thing in the universe exists because something else made it or produced it somehow. Everything in the material universe owes its existence to something else. That's what he means by contingent being. Let's take a simple example. I came into existence because my mother carried me to term. Before that, she and my father had sex, so did their parents, and so on. In my case, no Sam and Trudy, no Jake. In Thomas's view, if each natural being is contingent then the whole natural world is contingent. Something had to bring the universe into existence, something that has always existed and cannot pass out of existence. Philosophers and theologians call that Necessary Being (in contrast to Contingent Being), and Thomas identifies that being with God.

Now this is a very rough and admittedly simplified explanation of Thomas's argument. I don't suggest that it should demonstrate to you once and for all that God exists. Instead, I shared Thomas's reflections on contingency with you so that I can now encourage you to take a conceptual turn with me. You see, I believe that Thomas was right to glimpse a connection between our experience of the frail and fleeting nature of all things and God. Except, my philosophical lenses were shaped early on by the Existentialists. Under the influence of thinkers like Soren Kierkegaard, Martin Heidegger, Albert Camus, and Jean-Paul Sartre, I look within my own lived experience to grasp the meaning of contingency. My own personal contingency. I am mortal, as are you. Christians believe that an unflinching reflection on our mortality can yield an awareness that we receive our existence from beyond ourselves. We are not self-sustaining. We could not have brought ourselves into existence. And once we die, there's no pulling ourselves out of the grave by our own bootstraps. We Christians face our deaths squarely in order to see for ourselves that we—you and I along with every gnat, red giant star, duckbill platypus, and head of red leaf lettuce—derive our existence from *something* beyond us that is infinitely greater than ourselves. We receive life from *someone* who exercises a universe-creating power. That power is love. The divine love. For me, and for many of us, that insight is nurtured by Scripture, especially the creation narratives.

Most commentators agree that there are two originally distinct creation stories in the opening chapters of Genesis. For Christians, the narrative in chapter 1 recounts how God created the world in six days and rested on the seventh. We will circle back to this one—and its connection to John's Gospel—in the next section of this chapter. For now, we'll talk about the second story. There we hear how God imparts life to dust: "The Lord God formed man from the dust of the ground and breathed into his nostrils the breath of life, and the man became a living being" (Genesis 2:7). God gets down on hands and knees, makes a human-shaped pile of dirt, and then breathes into the human form's nose. Linger on this image for a moment. Yes, it's playful and a little comical. But importantly, it's intimate. God is present in the very breath we breathe. Every time we breath, we are reminded that God is with us. Some preachers and theologians teach that we call out the name of God every time we take a breath. They have in mind what is called the tetragrammaton. In some Bibles you may have seen God referred to as "Lord." That is actually a translation of the unpronounceable name of God, unpronounceable because it is too holy to utter: YHWH. In Hebrew, these letters are pronounced "Yod, Hey, Vav, Hey." These are aspirations. When you intone them, you can see that they resemble the simple act of breathing.

We are dust. Dust that calls the name of God by simply breathing. We are dust that lives. And this passage tells us that we receive the gift of life from a source beyond ourselves. Dust cannot give itself breath. Moreover, we get that breath in a tender, up-close-and-personal act of care. We are radically dependent upon a being for whom matter matters and whose very nature is to bring dust to life. In other words, this creation narrative suggests that every breath we take is a reminder of our intimate connection with a loving God. That we are God's beloved. Recognizing that we are the Beloved shapes how we navigate this planet and how we face death. God has put us here on purpose for a purpose, and that is crucial for leading a full-hearted life. But I've gotten ahead of myself. To be clear, we will need to discuss how the Incarnation—how the birth of Jesus—is a continuation of the creation story. So next we're going to look at how the Gospel of John amplifies the first creation story of Genesis.

## Beloved Dust

The opening words of the first page of the Bible are "in the beginning" (Genesis 1:1 KJV). Chapter 1 of Genesis goes on to tell the story of God speaking things into existence. God says, "Let there be . . ." and there is light and then dry land, sun and moon, plants and animals, and finally human beings. John's Gospel intentionally echoes that text and amplifies its message this way: "In the beginning was the Word, and the Word was with God, and the Word was God. He was in the beginning with God. All things came into being through him, and without him not one thing came into being" (John 1:1-3a). For some Christians, the coming of Jesus represents a course correction for the Creation. Their account goes something like this. In the beginning, God created the world, and it was good. The garden of Eden was perfect. However, Adam and Eve (either literally or figuratively) sinned and shattered the seamless connection between God and themselves. As a result, all of humanity would suffer an infinite disconnect from the Creator. To repair the breach, God sent Jesus. His life, death, and resurrection were God's Plan B for the universe. Jesus is God's response to human sin.

However, John's Gospel encourages a different take on the relationship between Creation and the Incarnation. The Word was in the beginning. Jesus was not a late-breaking contingency plan for a creation gone wild. On the contrary, medieval theologian and philosopher John Duns Scotus (1265/66–1308) argued that Jesus was God's first thought in the creation. God did not send Jesus to rescue the creation after it came apart at the seams. God created the universe to be in relationship with God through Jesus. "All things came into being through him." Or as Paul put it, "He is the image of the invisible God, the firstborn of all creation, for in him all things in heaven and on earth were created, things visible and invisible, whether thrones or dominions or rulers or powers—all things have been created through him and for him. He himself is before all things, and in him all things hold together" (Colossians 1:15-17). God's initial plan was to be in intimate relationship with, in union with, the creation. Jesus is God incarnate. Fully human and fully divine. In Jesus, Creator and

Creation are in a seamless, mysterious union. God envisioned and accomplished in Jesus an intimate, infinite embrace with us from the start. And in Jesus we see what it really means to be human. We are God's beloved dust. God's love, not our own list of achievements, is the source of our worth. Even though he's not a theologian, Bruce Springsteen makes the point in down-to-earth terms.

Springsteen is a mega celebrity. He's a world-renowned performer with loads of hits. Many of his songs are considered rock classics. To his kids? Bruce and his wife, Patti Scialfa, are just the parents; loving, supportive people. But still just parents. Springsteen put it this way in a 2017 *New York Times* interview: "[Our children] showed a healthy disinterest in our work over all the years. . . . They had their own musical heroes, they had their own music they were interested in. They'd be pretty blank-faced if someone mentioned a song title of mine."[25] Springsteen seems to realize that parents are meant to be their kids' fans, to applaud the kids on *their* stages, not the other way around. That's good for the now-young-adult Springsteen kids. And it's especially good for Bruce and Patti. They seem to have fended off the worst effects of celebrity. They recognize that they are more than—and in very positive ways less than—the image applauded by adoring fans, and more than their skills and their accomplishments. They've retained or recovered or simply remembered their authentic humanity. Springsteen was not writing his memoir and has not written his songs with Christian discipleship explicitly in mind. And yet, in much of his music he highlights the dignity of people who work hard to make ends meet when the odds are stacked against them. He reminds us to look for the dignity of every human being, especially in messy circumstances. That includes remembering our own enduring value. His capacity to do that rests upon his spiritual beliefs and on his awareness of his own finite, gritty humanity.

---

25. John Pareles, "Bruce Springsteen on Broadway: The Boss on His 'First Real Job,'" *New York Times*, September 27, 2017, https://www.nytimes.com/2017/09/27/arts/music/bruce-springsteen-broadway.html#:~:text=Just%20for%20your%20kids%20—%20your,music%20they%20were%20interested%20in.

Springsteen's memoir brings to mind another writer with a very different sort of celebrity. Henri Nouwen authored dozens of books on Christian spirituality. He taught at prestigious universities. Groups around the world sought after him as a speaker. By his own admission, Nouwen had come to identify himself with his intellectual power, his status as a widely read writer, and his authority as a respected academic. His feelings of self-worth depended upon the quality and quantity of his accomplishments and the continued relevance of his abilities. At the age of fifty-four he left his faculty position at Harvard and joined the staff of a community devoted to serving people with profound developmental disabilities. The residents of L'Arche Daybreak reminded Nouwen of his true humanity and of the roots of genuine discipleship. Nouwen writes, "The first thing that struck me when I came to live in a house with mentally handicapped people was that their liking or disliking me had absolutely nothing to do with the many useful things I had done until then. Since nobody could read my books, the books could not impress anyone."[26]

In other words, his many publications, his reputation as a writer and speaker, and his powers of insight were good. But he was both more and less than all of this. His significance as a human being derived from elsewhere. He writes, "These broken, wounded, and completely unpretentious people forced me to let go of my relevant self—the self that can do things, show things, prove things, build things—and forced me to reclaim that unadorned self in which I am completely vulnerable, open to receive and give love regardless of any accomplishments."[27]

The first step in living a full-hearted life is to acknowledge and reclaim this "unadorned self"; our true humanity. Paradoxically, that's precisely when we discover our infinite worth, our inalienable dignity as human beings. Every human being is the Beloved because God loves us. Period. And disciples are called by Jesus and sent into

---

26. Henri Nouwen, *In the Name of Jesus: Reflections on Christian Leadership* (New York: Crossroads), 27.

27. Nouwen, *In the Name of Jesus*, 28.

the world by him to deliver that one, life-transforming message. We were made by love for love. Turning again to Nouwen: "The great message that we have to carry, as ministers of God's Word and followers of Jesus, is that God loves us not because of what we do or accomplish, but because God has created and redeemed us in love and has chosen to proclaim that love as the true source of all human life."[28]

## Spiritual Reflections and Exercises

1. Meditate on this passage. "So teach us to count our days that we may gain a wise heart" (Psalm 90:12). How does counting your days—reflecting on your own mortality—affect you? What insights does this reflection give you about what is and is not important in your life? What would it mean to you to spend the time you have well?

2. Have you ever felt like what you were doing is fruitless or pointless? How did that affect your motivation and your sense of worth? How did you seek a sense of meaning?

3. What would you say if someone asked, "Are you afraid to die?"

4. If you believe in God, has that belief shaped your experience of grief? If you do not believe, how might a belief in God change your experience of grief?

5. Christians say that everyone is a beloved child of God. Does that make sense to you? Have you ever experienced yourself as infinitely loved and valued? Talk about a time when you experienced yourself as the Beloved. Talk about a time when you couldn't feel that way.

---

28. Nouwen, *In the Name of Jesus*, 30.

6. Recovering what Nouwen calls the unadorned self is at the root of the full-hearted life. That involves radical vulnerability. Talk or write about being vulnerable. Is it hard for you? Does it come easily? Talk about an experience of being vulnerable with God; with another person.

*Prayer*: Holy and merciful God, Creator of all things, help me to give myself back to you just as I am, without pretense and without fear. And then help me to give myself completely to your purposes in the assurance of your love. In Jesus's name. Amen.

*Tell me, what is it you plan to do with your one
wild and precious life?*

—Mary Oliver,
"The Summer Day"

Chapter Four

# The Resurrection-Shaped Self

IT'S CUSTOMARY FOR CLERGY to greet worshippers as they're leaving church. The people often say something to us about the sermon we preached that day. I've heard a range of things. "Good words, preacher." "You were talking right to me this morning." "You really made me think." It's rare to hear a criticism at the door. But a few negative comments have landed in my inbox during the following week or even a few months later. One of those email responses went something like this. "I owe you a debt of gratitude for that heretical Easter sermon. That's what finally convinced me to leave your church for another denomination."

As you might imagine, the theme of that Easter sermon was the Resurrection. That's a complex topic for a peculiarly challenging occasion. On Easter you can count on people showing up who last attended on Christmas (or maybe even several Easters ago). Kids are all dressed up and fueled by chocolate from the Easter egg hunt. Parents and grandparents are often more focused on the family gathering than on the mysteries of the faith. So, my rule of thumb for Easter is to keep it simple and to keep it short. In other words, make one point and sit down. The single point I sought to make that Easter Day is that the Resurrection is not just a resuscitation. Lazarus was resuscitated. He was brought back from the dead and would inevitably die again. Jesus was not merely brought back from the dead like Lazarus. He passed through death to eternal life—a life untouched by death, pain, and sorrow. And he came to give that kind of life to us.

My unhappy listener somehow heard me saying that the Resurrection didn't really happen. In fairness, aiming to make the distinction between resurrection and resuscitation might have been too ambitious during a service fraught with distractions. And I regret that my point was unclear to this person. That's because that distinction is crucial for understanding not only what Jesus's resurrection was but also for understanding what the power of the Resurrection is doing in our lives right now. Resurrection is God's love making us a new creation, now and in the afterlife. In this life, the Resurrection makes us who we truly are and shows us how to be true to ourselves in our daily lives. And as we'll see, that resurrection-shaped self participates in the kind of life that stretches beyond the grave into eternity. However, we cannot adequately discuss the Resurrection without first reflecting on the cross. The cross and the empty tomb cannot be separated. One of my favorite prayers puts it this way:

> Almighty God, whose most dear Son went not up to joy but first he suffered pain, and entered not into glory before he was crucified: Mercifully grant that we, walking in the way of the cross, may find it none other than the way of life and peace.[29]

## The Passion of Christ

During Holy Week Christians in liturgical churches like my own Episcopal Church turn our attention to the suffering and death of

---

29. The Book of Common Prayer (New York: Church Publishing Incorporated, 1979), 99.

Jesus. Our devotions begin on what we call Palm Sunday. In worship we remember that Jesus intentionally rode into Jerusalem on the back of a donkey. Waving palm leaves in celebration, large crowds enthusiastically greeted him as the Messiah. Matthew explains that Jesus was fulfilling Zechariah's prophecy: "Look, your king is coming to you, humble, and mounted on a donkey, and on a colt, the foal of a donkey" (Matthew 21:5 from Zechariah 9:9).

Commentators have pointed out that Jesus's entry into the holy city contrasted sharply with the Roman triumph.[30] The triumph was a parade celebrating a military victory. The commanding general entered the city and rolled through its streets in a four-horse chariot. His troops, his soon-to-be-enslaved captives, and the spoils of war trailed behind him. Wearing a crown of laurel and a gold-embroidered purple toga, the commanding officer was hailed as a sort of demi-god and a king-for-a-day. At least for that moment, he was immeasurably superior to all the ordinary slobs cheering and clapping along the parade route. The Roman triumph—and the imperial rule it represented—was based on the violent spilling of blood. By entering Jerusalem on the back of a humble work animal, Jesus demonstrated that he was one of us, not a condescending superior. His parade announced the reign of the humble king who was making the long-awaited kingdom of heaven into an earthly reality. That king wields the power of love. And he exercises that power not by spilling an enemy's blood, but by pouring out his own. He gives his blood, his life, for the healing of the world.

Listening to the Passion narrative read aloud in the worship service takes me to a solemn place. And yet it's the hymns we sing that grip me, that draw me viscerally into Jesus's humiliation, torture, and death. Maybe music moves you in a similar way, and you've been touched by great pieces like Bach's *St. Matthew Passion*. But Jesus encourages us to be more than compassionate or grateful or

---

30. Marcus Borg and John Dominic Crossan, *The Last Week: A Day-by-Day Account of Jesus' Final Week in Jerusalem* (San Francisco: Harper-One, 2006).

guilt-ridden spectators of what he has done. He wants us to follow him. To be transformed by his Passion into participants in the mending, liberating, reconciling work of the cross and resurrection. Jesus himself told us that following him means to take up our cross. The path to the empty tomb passes through Golgotha, the place where Jesus was crucified.

Paradoxically, for Christians the way to eternal life is to live fully and completely in this world. To embrace the contradictions of this life with unflinching realism. Our world is a mixture of joy and terror, delight and heartache, pleasure and pain. When Jesus stretched out his arms on the cross, he encompassed it all. He embraced the tensions and the conflicts of our existence. It is so very human to chase the delights and to flee the pain. But Jesus invites us to be in solidarity with the world's pain. This is not a command or a rule to follow. It's a vocation. A calling we may choose to follow. You see, Jesus knew that suffering afflicts everyone and distorts our lives. Each one of us will have to deal with our pain and suffering in some way or another. How we deal with our own pain is how we begin to deal with the world's suffering. All too often we humans have converted our pain into violence. We've either offloaded that pain onto others or turned it against ourselves in various forms of self-loathing. In either case, we have succeeded only in increasing the total pool of suffering.

Jesus offers a different way, what Richard Rohr calls a cruciform life. When the ache of the world enters this kind of life—when the pain of poverty, mass shootings, hunger, homelessness, racism, and homophobia haunts our own souls, breaks our own hearts, wounds our own bodies—it transforms us. We each move from being a wounded person to what Henri Nouwen famously called a wounded healer. Our focus has broadened to include not only our own private wounds, but the woundedness of the world. We are propelled by love to seek justice. Not punitive justice. Restorative justice. The justice that heals and mends the very source of our pain with the power of love. Here's how Richard Rohr puts it, "[Christians] agree to embrace the imperfection and even the injustices of our world, allowing these situations to change [us] from the inside out, which is the only way things are changed anyway."[31]

God's love makes suffering the birthplace of eternal life. The way of the cross already points to the empty tomb. It is in suffering that we can realize most clearly that we are unconditionally loved and that love makes life worth living. Rohr put it this way, "If all of our human crucifixions are leading to some possible resurrection, and are not dead-end tragedies, this changes everything. If God is somehow participating in our human suffering, instead of just passively tolerating it and observing it, that also changes everything."[32] In other words, when we are open to it, the divine compassion transforms us—not just in the next life, but already in this life. To echo Paul, we become a new creation in Christ (2 Corinthians 5:17). As we'll see below, being true to our relationship with the crucified and risen Jesus is how we remain true to ourselves and lead a full-hearted life.

## Who Am I Really?

Being true to who we are is crucial to human existence. And to be true to yourself you have to ask the question, who am I really? Christians form our identity in relationship with the crucified and risen Christ. Answering the call to follow Jesus allows us at once to be our individual selves and to be formed by our participation in a beloved community. We will discuss this at length in a moment. But first it's important to outline an alternative path to identity formation taken by many people in our culture. The sociologist Robert Bellah called it "expressive individualism"; it can leave us with a

31. Richard Rohr, *The Universal Christ: How a Forgotten Reality Can Change Everything We See, Hope for, and Believe* (New York: Convergent Books, 2019), 148.

32. Richard Rohr, "The Crucified Jesus," Center for Action and Contemplation, October 21, 2016, https://cac.org/daily-meditations /the-crucified-jesus-2016-10-21/.

tension between being an individual and belonging to something greater than ourselves. Glenn Close articulates the path of expressive individualism in her acceptance speech for the 2019 Golden Globe Best Actress in a Motion Picture (Drama) award.

Close had portrayed Joan Archer, the main character in the movie *The Wife*. Joan was a gifted writer, but the sexism of the literary world prevented her from establishing herself as an author. Instead, for public consumption she had played the role of supportive wife and muse for her celebrated novelist husband, Joseph, when in fact she was the ghostwriter for all of his books. When the Nobel Committee awarded him its coveted prize for literature, Joan went completely unrecognized. During their trip to Stockholm for the Nobel ceremony, Joan struggles with the decisions she's made about how to lead her life. Close shared that Joan's story had struck a personal chord. Her mother, Bettine, had devoted her life to supporting her husband's career. Looking back on her long life, Bettine confided to her daughter, "I feel like I haven't accomplished anything."[33] Playing the role of wife and mother, Bettine had given up the chance to make something of her own life. Of course, she loved her husband and her children, but she had expressed it in a way that meant setting aside her own passions and ambitions. As a result, she felt that she had not been true to herself. And that decision had left her with the sense that she had misspent the time she had been given; that she was insignificant. Close went on to say, "We have to find personal fulfillment. We have to follow our dreams. We have to say, 'I can do that, and I should be allowed to do that.'"[34]

Close's acceptance speech embodies the concept of self that underlies expressive individualism. What makes you "you" is that

33. Julie Kosin, "Glenn Close Gives Emotional, Rousing Golden Globes Acceptance Speech," *Harper's Bazaar*, January 6, 2019, https://www.harpersbazaar.com/culture/film-tv/a25770458/glenn-close-golden-globes-acceptance-speech/.

34. Kosin, "Glenn Close Gives Emotional, Rousing Golden Globes Acceptance Speech."

unique, inner core that each person possesses. Within you and within me lie desires, ambitions, abilities, and dreams. To be true to ourselves means to acknowledge and to express that inner core in our outward lives. We will make ourselves or lose ourselves through our choices. This is frequently called authenticity. And being authentic takes both work and courage. That's because society seeks to constrain our behavior—and hence impose a false self upon us—by forcing us into predefined roles that require us to suppress our own inner impulses. We betray our true self and abandon our need for self-fulfillment when we conform to society's expectations.

Expressive individualism puts us in an existential bind. Being an individual—taking responsibility for our own existence—is surely crucial to being your true self. And yet, so too is belonging to something greater than yourself. And belonging frequently requires sacrifice. I am a husband to Joy and a father to my kids, a bishop in the Episcopal Church, and a citizen of the United States. If I were just playing a role that I could easily shed, I could walk away from any of these communities without the slightest regret. But in crucial ways my marriage, my calling, and my social location have shaped me into who I truly am. I'm not wearing a mask as Joy's husband or as a pastor to the people of Louisiana. They've gotten under my skin, as it were. To love them, to serve them, and to walk through life together with them is an important part of who I am. Walking away or shirking my duties and responsibilities—even to pursue something I would love to do or to accomplish—would be more than a betrayal of them. It would also be a betrayal of my true self. Personal identity, it seems, requires both self-expression and self-sacrifice. And yet expressive individualism puts them in tension with each other.

John's account of the Resurrection teaches us that our personal identity emerges from our relationship with the risen Jesus (John 20:1-18). There we read about Mary Magdalene's initial meeting with the risen Jesus. In that encounter Mary receives a new sense of who she is. Let me explain. When Mary first arrives at the tomb, her world has been shattered. She was a loyal, enthusiastic follower of

Jesus. Following Jesus meant more than ascribing to a set of beliefs or pursuing a common cause. Jesus called his followers friends, and it's reasonable to assume that this bond of affection went both ways. Mary's identity was bound up with her relationship with Jesus. And then Jesus died on a cross and was buried. On the third day she comes to the tomb expecting to grieve a fallen friend. Instead, she finds an empty tomb. She assumes that someone has robbed the grave. So she rushes to find the Apostles and to report the body's disappearance. Peter and John rush to the burial site, Mary hot on their heels. They confirm her report and leave. She lingers. That's when a gardener asks her, "Whom are you looking for?" Those of us reading the Gospel know that the gardener is actually the risen Jesus. Mary just can't recognize him. Jesus then speaks her name, "Mary." The sound of her name, spoken tenderly, opens her eyes. "Rabbouni!" she says. "Teacher! It's you." She recognizes her friend. And then Jesus says what is for this context the crucial bit: "Do not touch me." In other words, "Don't cling to the Jesus that you knew previously." This Jesus has passed through death to an eternal kind of life. He is a new creation. Moreover, don't hold on to your old self. In other words, Mary is in for yet another soul stretching. Her relationship with the risen Jesus has become the source of her personal identity. And so it is with all of us who follow Jesus. The Resurrection shapes who we really are and what it means to be true to ourselves.

Jesus shows us a way to be ourselves that combines both self-sacrifice and self-expression. But crucially the source of our sense of who we are and what makes life meaningful is neither the society beyond us nor the private desires and impulses within us. Our identity and our self-worth emerge from our living relationship—our friendship—with the risen Christ (John 15:15). We become who we truly are neither by playing a role imposed upon us by society nor by expressing our inmost desires. Our true self emerges from accepting the risen Jesus's offer of friendship. The late philosopher and civil rights activist Howard Thurman once compared being true to yourself to responding to a voice that we hear calling from within us. Speaking to the 1980 graduates of Spelman College, he said, "There is something in every one of you that waits, listens for the genuine in yourself—and if you cannot hear it, you will never find whatever it is for which you are searching."[35] I take that "genuine" within us to be Jesus's invitation to friendship, a friendship in which we become who we truly are. As Thurman writes elsewhere, "Of course God cares for the grass of the field, which lives a day and is no more, or the sparrow that falls unnoticed by the wayside. He also holds the stars in their appointed places, leaves his mark in every living thing. And he cares for me!"[36] To be a disciple of Jesus Christ is to allow ourselves to be shaped by his relentless love for us into who we truly are: the Beloved.

Let's use Hartmut Rosa's concept of resonance to illustrate how our identity emerges from our relationship with the risen Jesus. In physics the term "resonance" describes the transfer of energy between objects. A common example is the interaction between tuning forks. If you put two tuning forks of the same frequency next to each other and then strike one of them, the second tuning fork begins to vibrate. Rosa adapts this concept from physics to describe how relationships shape and guide our lives. Resonance involves four characteristics. First, there is the sense of being "reached, touched or moved" inwardly by something beyond us. We are *affected*. Something "calls to us," addresses us. Think of being transported by a piece of music or stopped in your tracks by a sunset. That's when we say things like "Wow!" Our heart, our soul, our mind, even our body resonates with an Other. However, the spiritual vibrations within us are not merely involuntary reactions. We are not billiard balls set in motion by a collision with the cue ball. Resonance involves *self-efficacy*. We respond intentionally. It's like having that vague sense that someone is looking at us. Instead of ducking our

---

35. Howard Thurman, "The Sound of the Genuine," https://thurman .pitts.emory.edu/items/show/838.

36. Howard Thurman, *Jesus and the Disinherited* (Boston: Beacon Press, 1976), 46.

heads or looking away, we decide to return the gaze. I am not only seen. I see that I am being seen. And so too does the Other. Our interior lives are braided together. And that changes who we are. We undergo an *adaptive transformation*. Who we are—our sense of self—is evolving as a function of this relationship. Finally, it would be a mistake to chase resonance as if it were an achievement to be attained. There's an *uncontrollability* about resonance. We can't make it happen by force of will or conjure it up with some special skill set that we could learn from a resonance expert. It's not an achievement that we could strive to attain. Resonance is a gift that is given to us unlooked for.[37] It's more like the burning bush than a most valuable player trophy. God approached Moses on Mount Sinai in a way that only God could pull off and to which only Moses could respond.

As a result of our friendship with the risen Jesus, we know ourselves as the Beloved. And so, the only way to be true to ourselves is to love one another as Jesus has loved us. As Frederick Buechner says, "To be his friends . . . we have to be each other's friends, conceivably even lay down our lives for each other. You never know (John 15:12-15). It is a high price to pay, and Jesus does not pretend otherwise, but the implication is that it's worth every cent."[38] Jesus never promised to give us a pain-free ride on planet earth. As I've written elsewhere, "Life is not about being endlessly carefree. It's about being unguardedly, relentlessly caring."[39] Love like this makes us vulnerable to the suffering of others and can bring with it bruises to body and soul. However, love like this is also how we participate in a life that cannot be contained by any grave.

---

37. Hartmut Rosa, *The Uncontrollability of the World* (New York: Polity Press, 2020), 33–37.

38. Frederick Buechner, from *Whistling in the Dark*, in "Friends," September 26, 2016, https://www.frederickbuechner.com /quote-of-the-day/2016/9/26/friends.

39. Jake Owensby, *A Resurrection Shaped Life: Dying and Rising on Planet Earth* (Nashville: Abingdon Press, 2018), 103.

## See You Down the Road

Standing on his back porch, Dave raised his hand to say good-bye as I turned my Jeep's ignition. Our eyes met for a few moments, then I started the long ride home. A few days earlier, Dave's wife, Doris, had called to tell me that he had pancreatic cancer. The doctors thought he had just a few weeks. So I cleared my calendar and drove across three states to spend some time with my friend. We passed a day laughing, talking, and gazing silently out the windows of his sunroom. He noted that the hay fields needed to be harvested. Around noon we shared a simple lunch of homemade corn chowder and freshly baked bread. Eventually he got around to reflecting on his approaching death. As I was driving home from our visit, I found myself reflecting on what Jesus had said to his friends on their last night together: "Do not let your hearts be troubled. Believe in God; believe also in me" (John 14:1).

Jesus was preparing his friends for his own death. And he was also telling them that love is the key to living a full-hearted life in a world where the ones who love us, and the ones we love most, will die. This in a world where each one of us will die. Paradoxically, we learn about the power of the risen Jesus in our lives when we befriend our own mortality. That's what Dave did. As his disease progressed, he began to sense his mortality in his bones. Not as pain but as a sort of visceral wisdom. He saw each breath as an expression of God's love for him. The beating of his heart murmured, "Love is at work here." From one perspective, our mortality is a brute biological fact. We have a chronological sell-by date. Our EEG will eventually go flat. But with reflection we can discover in our finitude an essential spiritual lesson. As we discussed in the previous chapter, our lives are not self-sustaining. To exist, we draw sustenance from a source beyond ourselves.

You may have heard people say that we come into this life alone and that we leave it alone. And between our beginning and our end we're on our own to make something of ourselves. But Jesus teaches us that this is an illusion. God's love is not a long-distance affection. It's an intimate union. In the risen Jesus, God has braided together the human and the divine. Right down to the core of our being, *who* we are emerges from our intimate connection with God. Later in that final evening with his friends, Jesus put it like this: "Abide in me as I abide in you. Just as the branch cannot bear fruit by itself unless it abides in the vine, neither can you unless you abide in me. I am the vine; you are the branches. Those who abide in me and I in them bear much fruit, because apart from me you can do nothing" (John 15:4-5). Death cannot sever a connection like that. Neither can suffering or sorrow. As Paul famously said, "Who will separate us from the love of Christ? Will affliction or distress or persecution or famine or nakedness or peril or sword? . . . I am convinced that neither death, nor life, nor angels, nor rulers, nor things present, nor things to come, nor powers, nor height, nor depth, nor anything else in all creation will be able to separate us from the love of God in Christ Jesus our Lord" (Romans 8:35, 38-39). Ultimately, acknowledging our death teaches us decisively who we truly are. It teaches us that we are the Beloved, the one held in an infinite and eternal embrace by the risen Christ. We're true to ourselves when we give that love away with abandon.

Some will tell you that love breaks your heart. And while love can bring with it sorrow and confusion and frustration, it does not finally break our hearts. That's because the love we give is the love we have received from God. That love cannot be obliterated. When the ones we love pass from this plane—and when our own time comes—the power of love means that we never have to say goodbye. We can just say, "I'll see you down the road."

## Spiritual Reflections and Exercises

1. An elevator speech is a thirty-second summary of an idea. Give the elevator speech of who you are.

2. In which of your activities do you feel most "you"? What abilities make it possible for you to do that? Now imagine

giving that ability away or simply losing it? For example, if you're a teacher you lose your voice. From where might you receive a sense of identity and self-worth?

3. Try a similar exercise with your accomplishments. Which of your achievements do you want people to acknowledge and respect? Now imagine that times have changed, and nobody cares about those achievements anymore or that they are completely forgotten. From where might you receive a sense of identity and self-worth?

4. Does the idea of having a personal relationship with the risen Jesus make sense to you? If not, talk about why. If so, talk about what such a relationship means to you.

5. Have you ever seen yourself as a new creation? Tell that story.

*Prayer*: Almighty God, whom truly to know is everlasting life: Grant us so perfectly to know your Son Jesus Christ to be the way, the truth, and the life, that we may steadfastly follow his steps in the way that leads to eternal life; through Jesus Christ your Son our Lord, who lives and reigns with you, in the unity of the Holy Spirit, one God, for ever and ever. Amen.[40]

---

40. The Book of Common Prayer, 225.

*[The Holy Spirit] gives us the courage not to screen out those bits of the human world that are difficult, unpleasant, those that are not edifying. It opens our eyes and our ears and our hearts to the full range of what being human means.*

—Rowan Williams,
*Being Human: Bodies, Minds, Persons*

Chapter Five

# The Spirit of the Full-Hearted Life

NEIL ARMSTRONG STEPPED OUT of the Apollo 11 lunar module onto the moon's surface. The date was July 20, 1969. I was eleven years old. My mother and I watched Armstrong's "giant leap for mankind" on a black-and-white TV in a cheap motel room. Mom had spent most of her remaining cash to give us at least one night sleeping in a bed and a chance to see the lunar landing. We were homeless, having fled my physically and emotionally abusive father just a few weeks before. When we left, my mother had no job prospects, no savings, and no reliable support network. We carried with us two flimsy suitcases stuffed with our belongings. This is the sort of desperate gamble a mother will take when her husband points a gun at her and then puts that same pistol in her son's face.

Stretches of my life have been messy. How to navigate the way through them and the way forward from them was anything but clear. To be honest, I spent years being ashamed of my life's messiness. I supposed that everybody else had life pretty well figured out. They were normal, and messiness marked me as the oddball outsider. So, there was no chance that was I going to tell anybody about my abusive dad, or my experience of homelessness, or that by the time I had reached high school I had lived at seventeen different, often shabby, addresses. I struggled with who I was, how to act, and what to do with my life. Years of pastoral ministry have taught me that, at one time or another, most people find themselves in some pretty messy places. Your mess and my mess are probably different. But mess it is. Period. And most of us yearn for something to help us make sense of, and to navigate our way through, our own confusing, complex situations. For Jesus followers, that something is a someone. The Holy Spirit abides in the midst of our ordinary life as wise counselor and trustworthy friend. Jesus told us, "Out of the believer's heart shall flow rivers of living water" (John 7:38). Over time the Holy Spirit teaches us wisdom. And wisdom is the art of doing the ordinary and the extraordinary things of our life with love. And love is the essence of the full-hearted life.

## Love and Wisdom

My friend J. is the executive director of a nonprofit group that provides addiction recovery services to individuals, families, and organizations. We were both members of a task force charged by our denomination with responding to the nation's opioid crisis. At one of our meetings, we were all discussing the stress, the heartbreak, the chronic worry, and the agonizing choices facing the parents of addicted daughters and sons. The idea of tough love came up. On that view, parents should give their sons and daughters a clear choice. Get clean or get out. Offering financial support of any kind would enable and perpetuate what is a progressive and ultimately fatal disease. J. surprised me by encouraging us not to accept tough love as dogma. She said, "It's easy for a bystander to insist on it. But each parent has to ask this question for themselves: Am I willing to get that midnight knock at the door? The notification that my daughter or my son is dead. There's more than one right answer." In other words, there's more than one right way to approach addiction.

It struck me that what J. was saying about addiction goes for much of life in general. There's more than one right way. No two situations are exactly alike. Each individual brings a different set of intellectual, physical, and emotional strengths and weaknesses to every set of circumstances. Life is hard, complicated, and frequently baffling. And Jesus never gave us a list of dos and don'ts for every conceivable situation. Instead of telling us what to do in exhaustive detail, he told us *how* to do whatever it is we do. He said, "This is my commandment, that you love one another as I have loved you" (John 15:12). In other words, he tells us to do what we do with love. There is more than one right way to love. And our challenge is to find how best to love in all the more or less messy places of this life. That's where the Holy Spirit comes in. But before I say more about the Holy Spirit's role in our everyday life, let me be clear about something.

I'm not suggesting that right and wrong are relative. Good and evil are not up to each individual or a function of the culture we happen to live in. On the contrary, Jesus insisted that the moral law is universal. He said, "For truly I tell you, until heaven and earth pass away, not one letter, not one stroke of a letter, will pass from the law until all is accomplished" (Matthew 5:18).[41] But crucially, Jesus emphasized the importance of learning the spirit of the law: love God and love neighbor. He recognized that the human challenge is that the moral law gives us *general* principles. Each day presents us with very *specific* circumstances that give us more than one genuinely moral path to take. It's like this. I understand that Jesus teaches us to love. Period. But what does love look like when we're searching for the best way to respond to a relative who is struggling with an eating disorder, a mental illness, or an addiction? We might all like a manual; a set of rules to

---

41.   There is a range of interpretations about the meaning of the phrase "until all is accomplished." Anglicans like me usually offer a Christ-centered approach. Jesus's life and mission ultimately fulfill the purpose of the law.

follow. But what we actually need is wisdom. Here's how I have defined wisdom elsewhere: "Wisdom is the art of doing the loving, God-shaped thing in all the varied, changing, and nuanced situations that life hands us."[42] Or as I mentioned above, wisdom is the spirit of the full-hearted life.

There is no life hack for becoming a wise person. We acquire wisdom one step, one day, one messy situation at a time. It's that ten thousand–hour thing you might have heard about. You master an art like playing guitar, writing poetry, or kicking a soccer ball by doing it over and over and over. Acquiring wisdom takes ten thousand hours (or more like eternity). It also requires a mentor—someone to show you how to do the thing you're trying to master; someone who cares enough about you to stick with you, to be supportive, and also to be lovingly candid with criticism. When it comes to wisdom, the Holy Spirit is our primary teacher. As Paul put it, "[Jesus] became wisdom for us from God" (1 Corinthians 1:30). You'll find one of Jesus's most condensed and yet comprehensive wisdom lessons in what commentators often call the Sermon on the Plain (Luke 6:17-49). Jesus opens with a series of blessings (or beatitudes) and woes. The poor, the hungry, and the weeping are blessed. They possess the kingdom of God, will be filled, and will laugh. By contrast, the rich, the well-fed, and the carefree are in for eventual distress and heartbreak. This is Jesus's first principle in the wisdom curriculum. Some hear him saying that the former are God's favored group while the latter are in for judgment. Jesus, they believe, is drawing a moral distinction here.

And it does seem clear to me that Jesus has a thing for underdogs and outcasts and that he resists those who use other people like doormats to improve their own lot. But I also believe that he has another lesson for us here. Let me put it this way. Life is always changing and unpredictable. Try as best you can, you're not always going to get the results you want. Good intentions and hard work can still land you in a wrenching mess. Jesus wants us to

---

42. Jake Owensby, *Looking for God in Messy Places: A Book about Hope* (Nashville: Abingdon Press, 2021), 110.

know that, when we're flat on our face, he's still with us and that his loving presence will ultimately make a difference. At the same time, he also wants us to realize that, when we're on a roll, it's awfully easy to forget that we need God. It's best to keep in mind that things can go south with shocking speed. Besides, each of us gets only so much time on planet earth. So whether we are rich or poor, weeping or letting the good times roll, we need wisdom. Life inevitably gets messy. And wisdom is how we navigate messy places.

Farther along in the sermon, Jesus lays out the practices needed to grow in wisdom. We have to exercise these practices day in and day out. Sometimes we'll do them admirably well. With humbling frequency, our efforts will be flawed and halting. Here are some of the practices assigned in Jesus's wisdom school:

- Love your enemies, do good to those who hate you, bless those who curse you.
- Give to those who would rob you, give to all who beg.
- Be merciful, do not judge or condemn, forgive.

Life is complicated. Everybody is imperfect. And we are all in this together. Love is how we'll make this planet livable for us all. The Holy Spirit is guide and mentor, counselor and friend in the school of wisdom for everyday life.

## The Spirit of Friendship

To be clear about the Spirit as the source of wisdom, it's helpful to think of the Holy Spirit as our enduring friendship with the risen Jesus. To explain what I mean by this, I'm going to step you through some points of intersection between what Jesus says about the Holy Spirit and what the book of Proverbs teaches us about friendship. During the Last Supper Jesus said, "I do not call you servants any longer . . . but I have called you friends" (John 15:15).

He then went on to say, "You did not choose me, but I chose you" (John 15:16). In Proverbs, we read that a friend is different from a family member. You don't choose your siblings or your parents. They may be very supportive. Then again, they may not like you so much. Mostly they'll put up with you, but not always. By contrast, friendship is deliberate. A friend *chooses* to be your friend. The writer of Proverbs says, "A true friend sticks closer than one's sibling" (Proverbs 18:24).

Jesus described the Holy Spirit as an Advocate or a Helper. The Spirit will "teach you everything and remind you of all that I have said to you" (John 14:26). During his earthly ministry Jesus had been teaching his followers how to discern the loving thing to do—the God-inspired thing to do—in all the messy, varied, complex situations they would encounter. Proverbs calls that kind of discernment wisdom. None of us can exercise wisdom on our own. We need counsel. In fact, wisdom begins with the recognition that we need guidance to navigate this life: "The fear of the LORD is the beginning of wisdom" (Proverbs 9:10). The word *fear* in that passage means something like awe, the recognition that God is God, and we are not. And so, wise people recognize the limits of their own wit and the folly of stubborn self-reliance. They acknowledge their need for divine help to walk the way of love in this confusing, tumultuous world. As Proverbs tells us, "Trust in the LORD with all your heart, and do not rely on your own insight. In all your ways acknowledge him, and he will make straight your paths" (Proverbs 3:5-6).

In addition to giving us direction, a good counselor will also be honest with us when we've gone off the rails. A true friend will tell you those things that you would rather not hear. Hard truth may not be pleasant to receive, but it does more for our souls than flattery ever could. The writer of Proverbs puts it this way: "Well meant are the wounds a friend inflicts. . . . Iron sharpens iron, and one person sharpens the wits of another" (Proverbs 27:6, 17). Admittedly, some people will say intentionally hurtful things in the guise of telling the truth in love. Their real aim is to get in a dig without taking responsibility for the pain they cause. A genuine friend doesn't do this. And that's not how the Spirit operates. As Jesus said, "I have said these things to you so that my joy may be in you and that your joy may be complete" (John 15:11).

You see, the Spirit understands us from the inside. Jesus told his friends, "The Spirit of Truth . . . abides with you" (John 14:17). So we can be assured that the Spirit's counsel—even the most challenging counsel—comes from a place of infinite compassion. Here's how Proverbs describes a friend's counsel: "Perfume and incense bring joy to the heart, and the pleasantness of a friend springs from their heartfelt advice" (Proverbs 27:9 NRSV). A friend's counsel is "heartfelt." The Spirit's advice is always an expression of Jesus's love for us. Jesus assured his friends, "I will not leave you orphaned" (John 14:18). Whether the sailing is smooth or the seas are treacherous, whether we're on the top of our game or at a dismally low bottom, the Spirit is there. The Holy Spirit hangs with us, guides us, and leads us to the next step of the path we walk together. Again and again, the Spirit challenges us with life's two biggest questions. Oddly enough, I recognized those questions at the center of a popular television series that I streamed a couple of years ago.

## The Spirit's Two Big Questions

After *The Good Place* hit Netflix, I binge-watched the entire first season. Friends had been insisting that I would love it. After all, one of the main characters is an ethicist. How could a former philosophy professor like me resist it? In a way, my friends were right. The character Chidi Anagonye's brief lectures on Kant, Aristotle, and Utilitarianism did warm the nerdy corners of my heart. But what kept me glued to the screen was something else. As I saw it, the show consistently encouraged viewers to face two questions. As it turns out, they're the two questions that the Holy Spirit puts before us again and again:

- Who or what is your God?
- Who are you?

Not coincidentally, these are the very questions that Jesus faces as he wanders in the desert and wrestles with temptation. But I'm getting ahead of myself. You may not have seen *The Good Place* or your take on the show may be very different from mine. So here's my synopsis of the show's premise.

The main character—Eleanor Shellstrop—has died and finds herself in a waiting room. An official named Michael greets her and welcomes her to the Good Place, ostensibly heaven. It's a place where everyone will have a soulmate, everyone lives in their dream home, and every conceivable innocent pleasure is available just for the asking. Only the very best people gain admission to the Good Place. Michael beams as he reads aloud the list of Eleanor's humanitarian achievements and describes her selfless lifestyle. There's just one problem. He's reading the life-record of a different Eleanor. The Eleanor sitting in front of Michael was a self-absorbed, mean-spirited jerk. A celestial mistake has been made. This Eleanor belongs in the Bad Place. So Eleanor has to hide her true identity and, since the ethics prof turns out to be her soulmate, she goads him into giving her lessons that will help her at least appear good enough to stay in the Good Place before the authorities discover their mistake and ship her off to hell.

The series raises lots of questions about grace and judgment, good and evil, heaven and hell. But all of these questions turn, it seems to me, on the two more foundational questions that I've already mentioned:

- Who or what is your God?
- Who are you?

You see, Eleanor recognizes immediately that Michael has confused her with somebody else named Eleanor. As the episodes unfold, Eleanor struggles to face who she had been during her earthly life, but she also begins to undergo a transformation from selfishness to selflessness. We humans learn who we should love and how to love over time, even if it turns out to be a slow, uneven process. And in fact, the experiences that residents of the Good Place keep having make you reflect on the true nature of the good life. Soulmates take more work than you might have thought. Having a dream house seems empty. And having a million flavors of ice cream to choose from without worrying about gaining weight stops being a thrill pretty fast. Maybe paradise isn't all it's cracked up to be. For that matter, maybe a God whose primary role in human existence boils down to judging your worth and deciding your eternal fate is not a God worth worshipping. I mean, it seems to me that, if your God is worth worshipping, loving that God would lead to the sort of full-hearted life we've been talking about. By contrast, scurrying to score eternal pleasure and to avoid eternal misery sounds like a self-centered, anxiety-filled existence.

What on earth does any of this have to do with wisdom? Let's look at the connection between Jesus's baptism and his temptation in the wilderness. After John immersed Jesus in the waters of the Jordan, the Spirit descended upon him. A heavenly voice said, "You are my Son, the Beloved" (Luke 3:22b). Jesus hears that his vocation—his purpose in this world—derives from his identity as the Beloved. And then immediately the Spirit led him into the desert. In a manner of speaking, the Spirit sends Jesus on a forty-day retreat in order to get his messianic head on straight. The focus was to discern his calling with depth and clarity. The foundational questions for his, and for anyone's, sense of vocation are these:

- Who or what is your God?
- Who are you?

Satan's temptations challenge Jesus to ask these questions for himself. As it turns out, these questions are so interconnected that they have to be answered in concert. In this context, "God" is who or what we genuinely set our heart upon. What we as an individual pursue as our highest good. What we love above all else. We order all of our other wants and desires around that highest love. Which wants and desires will serve to bring us nearer to our love if we pursue them? Which of our yearnings should be sacrificed for that sake of a greater love? Who or what we love makes us who we truly are.

Our fidelity to that love—or our betrayal of it—shapes our lives and determines what we stand for.

Satan recognized that we can devote ourselves to counterfeit gods, so he tempted Jesus to elevate lesser loves—pleasure, power, and status—up to the level of highest love. He urged the hungry Jesus to turn stones into bread for his own comfort. Next, Satan offered the weary and weakened Jesus earthly power—a throne from which to rule the nations—in exchange for a little devil worship. Finally, Satan tempted Jesus with religious celebrity. He said something like: "Toss yourself off the steeple so everybody can see how spectacular God's favorite is" (Luke 4:1-12; see also Matthew 4:1-11). In other words, he tempted Jesus to indulge in idolatry. An idol is a phony god. It promises to satisfy our deepest, most enduring needs in exchange for absolute devotion. We want security, tranquility, and a sense of personal significance. And Satan tempts Jesus with idols that we are all too familiar with today: possessions, power, and status. Some people are consumed by the pursuit of wealth. But investments can lose value. So we're left with the nagging fear that we may not have enough and that we must secure more. Likewise, power can be used to keep us safe from danger. And yet paradoxically, the more we rely upon our own power to make us safe, the more energy we expend, and anxiety we experience, anticipating threats. Finally, status depends upon the applause of the crowd. As soon as it dies down, we have to chase the next ovation. And there's always the fear that we will become yesterday's news when the new It-person takes the stage. If your god is possessions or power or status, you are only what you can make of yourself with your stuff, your strength, or your achievements.

Jesus chooses a different way. He rejects these temptations and chooses to be who God makes him. Not who or what he can make of himself. Jesus takes the voice from heaven at its word. He is the Beloved. And only God can make him the Beloved. His calling in life is to live up to and into that divinely given identity for his own sake and for the sake of the world. Jesus recognized that his calling was to be the conduit or the instrument of God's love on this planet. Only love can make this shattered world whole again. Only

love can make this a good place where each person knows themselves as, and celebrates everyone they meet as, the beloved child of
God. As followers of Jesus, we have received that same calling: to
be the healing, liberating, nurturing ambassador of God's love. And
to lean into our calling, each and every one of us must face the same
questions that Jesus came to terms with: Who or what is your God?
Who are you? When we answer those questions honestly, we'll find
that the full-hearted life often means letting go—letting go not just
of what is bad, but of some good things that we love.


## Letting Go for Our Own Good

The Scottish sprinter Eric Liddell was favored to win the 100
meters at the 1924 Summer Olympics in Paris.[43] He decided not to
compete in the event. The qualifying heat fell on a Sunday. For him,
honoring the Sabbath precluded work of any kind, including running in a track meet. If you've seen the film *Chariots of Fire* (1981),
you know that Liddell ended up bringing home a gold medal. The
qualifying heat for the 400 took place on a weekday. So he switched
to that event and won in the final. By contrast, playing sports on
a Sunday is common now. Young athletes of every religious and
nonreligious type—chauffeured by their devoted, increasingly
exhausted parents—travel miles and miles to softball, lacrosse, soccer, and baseball tournaments that last for an entire weekend, week
after week.

Since I'm a bishop you might be expecting me to urge Christians
to follow Liddell's example and skip Sunday sports and go to church.
But that's not what I've got in mind here. Instead, I see in Liddell's
decision a reminder for all of us about what it means to live the

---

43.    Information about Eric Liddell is widely available on the
internet. See, for instance, https://www.britannica.com/biography/Eric
-Liddell; https://ericliddell.org/about-eric-liddell/; https://www.christianity
.org.uk/article/eric-liddell. See also the biography by David MacCasland,
*Eric Liddell: Pure Gold* (Grand Rapids: Discovery House, 2001).

full-hearted life that Jesus offers us. As Bonhoeffer famously put it, discipleship has a cost. We have to let some things go when we follow Jesus. And as it turns out, letting go is for our own good. Being a disciple is more than being a rule follower. It's about being defined by a relationship: by our relationship with the risen Christ. I can't say for sure, but I don't think that Liddell's decision to forgo the 100 was driven by a commitment to a principle like "Don't work on Sunday." He was committed to a person.

Liddell's real challenge was one that Jesus faced in the wilderness and that we all face at one time or another. What do I really base my life on? To what am I ultimately committed? For Christians, our ultimate commitment is to Jesus. So we ask, is there anything in my life that competes with my commitment to Jesus? Even and especially good things? If so, can I let that go? That's what Jesus is getting at with this shocking statement: "Whoever comes to me and does not hate father and mother, wife and children, brothers and sisters, yes, and even life itself, cannot be my disciple" (Luke 14:26).

Jesus was a devout Jew. He would never have forsaken the commandment to honor his parents. And the Prince of Peace is hardly going to advocate bearing a grudge and harboring ill will toward anybody. He even told us to love our enemies. However, he was clear that we tend to make good things into ultimate things. Family is a good thing. But it is not the ultimate thing. And if we ask our spouse or our children to be our ultimate thing, we place an unbearable burden upon them. For example, I love my wife. But she's not going to save me. Especially not from myself. My sons and my daughter mean the world to me. And yet if I were to tie my sense of self-worth to their achievements and success, I would spiritually suffocate them.

People let people down because, well, we're people. Mostly we mean well. But we don't really know the big picture. So even acting with the very best intentions can start a dumpster fire. Besides, each of us has only so much energy. We can't be everywhere all at once. And even if we could, we would bring our persistent quirks and flaws along with us. So Jesus taught us to love one another as the imperfect creatures that we are. He taught us to forgive one another and to seek reconciliation. An ultimate thing is the ultimate thing precisely because it will never let you down. It makes life worth living no matter what. No human can do that for us. Being a disciple means letting our relationship with Jesus be the ultimate thing. And when we do that, we can really love people as people, including ourselves.

As I've already mentioned, Jesus warns us especially about staking our lives on power, status, and wealth. Having some influence, being acknowledged for our achievements, and enjoying financial security are good things. But they are not ultimate things. That's why Jesus says, "None of you can become my disciple if you do not give up all your possessions" (Luke 14:33). To put it simply, none of this stuff will love you back. And if you love stuff above all else, you'll never really know what it's like to love another person. Everybody will be just a means to getting and keeping stuff. To genuinely enjoy the things of this world, we cannot treat them as our ultimate love. We have to let them go for our own good.

After the Olympics, Liddell went to serve as a missionary in China. When the Japanese army invaded, he was captured and put in a prison camp for civilians. He died there in 1945. Survivors of the camp reported that he was a powerful, sustaining spiritual presence in their midst. His death left a terrible hole in the surviving community. During the 2008 Beijing Olympics, the Chinese government claimed that Liddell had been offered release in a prisoner exchange. According to them, he declined the offer and gave his place to another prisoner: a pregnant woman. Soon afterward he died. The account of the exchange remains disputed. But this much is certainly true. Liddell had already defined his life with Christ as the ultimate thing. He was ready to give even his life away to be Jesus's disciple. Weakened by a brain tumor, he is said to have struggled to utter the word *surrender* with his last breath.

# Spiritual Reflections and Exercises

1. Describe what makes your most trusted friend your friend. Recall a story when you relied upon that friend for guidance or support.

2. Do you consider yourself a good friend? How have you shown your friendship to another?

3. Does calling Jesus your friend make sense to you? Have you experienced him that way?

4. Have you ever felt a spiritual presence in your life? Talk or write about what that was like. If you believe in the Holy Spirit, recall a time that the Holy Spirit guided, counseled, or simply accompanied you. What was the situation? Describe as best you can how you experienced the Spirit's presence.

5. Similar to many other spiritual traditions, walking the way of Jesus involves letting go. What would you struggle to let go of?

*Prayer*: Wise and loving God, I do not always see the path ahead of me clearly. I need your help to walk the way of Jesus. Give me ears to hear the Spirit's counsel, the humility to accept the Spirit's correction, and the trust to follow the Spirit's guidance. In the name of the loving, liberating, life-giving God. Amen.

## PART III

# FAITH IN PRACTICE

*We cannot attain the presence of God because we're already totally in the presence of God. What's absent is awareness.*

—Richard Rohr, *What the Mystics Know*

*But the hour is coming and is now here when the true worshipers will worship the Father in spirit and truth.*

—John 4:23

# Chapter Six

# Worship in Spirit and Truth

THE MOVERS HAD FINISHED UNLOADING the van well after sunset. So Joy and I waited until morning to start unpacking. I was looking for the box marked "coffee maker" when the phone rang. It was our Realtor S. He said, "I need to ask you a question." Assuming that this was some minor real estate thing, I distractedly said, "Well sure. What's up?" He answered, "What do I have to do to be saved?" He explained that he had long ago put spiritual stuff in the rearview mirror. His parents had given him a strict religious upbringing. Church had been an endless stream of talk about God's judgment, heaven, and especially hell. It was a total turnoff. Once he was paying his own bills and living under his own roof, he stopped giving religion any thought. But now he was in middle age. His daughter had reached her teens. His perspective on life had changed. The whole God thing had taken on a new significance. So he had recently started worshipping at the congregation that I would begin serving on the following Sunday. He wanted to know what else was required to be saved.

Like many people in the Deep South, S. was concerned about the afterlife, about avoiding hell and going to heaven. Getting right with God in this life was, in his mind, the key to securing the desired final destination. Obeying the moral law seemed like a no-brainer. But he also believed that he should be more spiritual to please God. Worship attendance was an obvious place to start. But he knew that the Christian life consists of other spiritual practices like prayer, Bible study, serving the poor, and the like. So he had reached out to me to learn which of these spiritual practices were most important and how to do them. Of course, practices are an essential part of Christian life, and I'm always happy to talk to people about them. However, practices are meant to nurture and enhance our life-defining spirituality. So, given the varied spiritual landscape we now inhabit, I think it's fruitful to begin with a conversation about spirituality in general.

Ronald Rolheiser argues that "what we do with our longings, both in terms of handling the pain and the hope they bring us, that is our spirituality."[44] That's why he goes on to say that "everyone has to have a spirituality and everyone does have one."[45] Longing is part of being human. So each of us is spiritual, whether we realize it or not. However, not all spiritualities are equal. How we habitually interpret and pursue our deepest yearnings will draw us closer to or distance us from the full-hearted life. Each spirituality will be "either a life-giving one or a destructive one."[46] What makes a Christian practice, well, authentically Christian is that participating in it nurtures and enhances our relationship with the risen Jesus. When an atheist recites Christian prayers or reads the Bible, something else is happening. It may in some way enhance their lives, but their intention is not to draw closer to Jesus. And that brings us back to S. The more I listened to him, the more I

---

44. Ronald Rolheiser, *The Holy Longing* (New York: Random House, 1998), 5.

45. Rolheiser, *The Holy Longing*, 6.

46. Rolheiser, *The Holy Longing*, 6.

came to believe that he was a functional atheist. Yes, he went to church and said his prayers and read the Bible. But his spirituality was functionally atheist. And he is not alone among contemporary churchgoers. On the contrary, in my pastoral experience I encounter it frequently. So in order to discuss how Christian spiritual practices foster a full-hearted life, let's begin by looking at the need to move beyond functional atheism.

## Beyond Functional Atheism

In his book *The Gay Science*, the philosopher Friedrich Nietzsche illustrates what I mean by "functional atheism" with a parable. It goes like this. There was once a madman who lit a lantern in the bright morning sun. He ran to the marketplace and shouted, "I'm looking for God!" The people shopping there laughed at the man and scoffed, "Is he lost? Is he hiding? Has he gone on vacation?" The madman whirled on them and said, "I'll tell you where he is! We've killed him, you and I."[47] The madman's accusation that *we* have killed God is the key to Nietzsche's parable. That is to say, a longing for the God of Abraham, Isaac, and Moses—a longing for a relationship with the risen Christ—no longer animates the lives of many people, even church-going, creed-professing people. Our life-shaping desire is no longer focused on the Transcendent God. Many lives—including the lives of self-identified Christians—are centered on things of this world. Functional atheism does not require anyone to deny the existence of God. It simply develops as a function of what we pursue in order to satisfy our deepest longings. And that's where Nietzsche's parable stings for so many of us. Even if you go to church, follow the Ten Commandments, and say a creed, you might just still be a functional atheist. "You

---

47. Friedrich Nietzsche, *The Gay Science: With a Prelude in Rhymes and an Appendix of Songs*, trans. Walter Kaufmann (New York: Vintage Books, 1974), Section 125.

have killed God," or replaced God with something less, without even realizing it. As Richard Rohr once said in an interview with Oprah Winfrey, "Religion is one of the safest places to hide from God."[48]

The philosopher John Gray argues that our secular age has witnessed the emergence of several kinds of atheism.[49] Only some of them are overtly anti-religious. In fact, I've observed that some of them can live very comfortably in a church's pews. You can devote yourself to a political identity, to social causes, or to beauty. For instance, Joy and I worshipped at Westminster Cathedral a few years back. An Englishwoman sitting next to us assured Joy, "I'm only here for the music." We can listen to sacred music—music composed to move the soul closer to the divine—merely for its aesthetic appeal. The author Derek Thompson argues that the most potent of these functional atheisms is workism. Here's how he defines it: "It is the belief that work is not only necessary to economic production, but also the centerpiece of one's identity and life's purpose."[50]

Career goals motivate us, and our achievements make us somebody. My concern for S. was that he remained deeply shaped by workism.

Let me be clear. Hard work can be a virtue. And doing something you love and doing it well can be richly rewarding. But workism is about more than industriousness and honing your skills. At its core, workism is a spirituality. It measures human value as a function of productivity and efficiency. Under workism's influence, we begin to assess our own worth and the value of our neighbors on the basis of their material success. Wealth becomes a status symbol, poverty a stigma. It would be impossible to live in

48. "Father Richard Rohr: The Universal Christ," Oprah's Super Sunday Podcast, June 3, 2019, https://www.oprah.com/own-podcasts/super-soul-special-father-richard-rohr-the-universal-christ.

49. John Gray, *Seven Types of Atheism* (New York: MacMillan, 2018).

50. Derek Thompson, "Workism Is Making Americans Miserable," *The Atlantic*, February 24, 2019, https://www.theatlantic.com/ideas/archive/2019/02/religion-workism-making-americans-miserable/583441/.

our culture and to have escaped entirely the influence of workism. The very core of the American dream is that hard work will lead to a better life. Where we go wrong is the assumption that our own worth is a result of our work and that others are due only the respect that they've earned.

Workism distorts worship, prayer, feeding the hungry, housing the hungry, and all spiritual practices into transactions. We engage in them to win God over. But that is not what Jesus teaches us. And his teaching begins with the recognition that we will probably need to change our life-defining focus. Here's how he put it: "The time is fulfilled, and the kingdom of God has come near; repent, and believe in the *good news*" (Mark 1:15, emphasis added).

The good news is that we are already the Beloved. Like any news, it reports what has already happened. We don't have to make ourselves worth loving. Jesus came to convince us that we are already loved. As Simone Weil puts it, "We cannot take a step toward the heavens. God crosses the universe and comes to us."[51] Spiritual practices are an essential part of the Christian life. But it's crucial to understand what they actually are. They are responses to the infinite love that God has always already given us, not pleas to receive what we do not have. So having said what spiritual practices are not, let's turn to a more in-depth look at what spiritual practices are.

## What Is a Spiritual Practice?

There are many traditional Christian spiritual practices: meditation, visiting the sick, fasting, sheltering the homeless, and Bible study. Anyone can do any of these things for a variety of good reasons. For instance, meditation is an increasingly popular technique

---

51. Simone Weil, *Waiting for God* (New York: Routledge Classics, 2021), 85.

for coping with the stresses and strains of hectic modern life. Apps on our phones and on our smart watches help us in our pursuit of an inner calm. Likewise, we might fast to lose weight or volunteer at a homeless shelter because we want to be better people. People do this stuff to improve themselves psychologically, physically, and morally. And there is nothing in the world wrong with that. For that matter, practices can have precisely this kind of effect for Christians. But our aim is not self-improvement. It's relationship. As I mentioned above, what makes a practice an authentic Christian practice is that our intention is to deepen our relationship with the crucified and risen Jesus. Personal prayer, almsgivings, and the like are our responses to the love that Christ is always already pouring out to us. Our primary motive is to open ourselves to that love. As Nora Gallagher writes: "To engage in a practice is to show up and not get attached to the outcome. . . . [The] purpose of a spiritual practice is to help us stay awake. Hidden in this kind of repetition is the chance that on any given day, the mind or the soul will connect with what is waiting to connect to us."[52] Spiritual practices connect us to God. Or more precisely, spiritual practices help us to be aware that God is always initiating connection with us. As Brian McLaren puts it, "Spiritual practices are ways of becoming awake and staying awake to God."[53]

The story of Zacchaeus has something to tell us about spiritual practices. Jesus was passing through Jericho. Zacchaeus joined the large crowd that gathered to see him. Since Zacchaeus was short, he climbed a tree to catch a glimpse of the rabbi. Jesus stops in his tracks, looks up at Zacchaeus, and says, "I'm coming to your place for dinner!" Every jaw in that crowd must have dropped. Zacchaeus was widely and perhaps understandably loathed by his neighbors. As a tax collector, he was a willing agent of the brutal Roman occupiers. Gallingly, their taxes paid for that occupation. And to make

---

52. Nora Gallagher, *The Sacred Meal.* Ancient Practices Series (Nashville: Thomas Nelson, 2009), loc. 121, Kindle.

53. Brian D. McLaren, *Finding Our Way Again.* Ancient Practices Series (Nashville: Thomas Nelson, 2008), 18.

matters worse, Zacchaeus followed the usual practice of enriching himself by heaping a surcharge onto the already burdensome tax bill. Zacchaeus welcomed Jesus into his house. He then pledged half of his wealth to the poor and promised to make amends to anyone he had defrauded. Jesus said, "Today salvation has come to this house" (Luke 19:9). The Zacchaeus narrative outlines the structure of spiritual practices. Crucially, Jesus initiates connection. People respond with not only an isolated act but with a pattern of living in the world. For instance, it's reasonable to imagine that Zacchaeus did more than make a one-time gift to a food pantry and pay off a handful of offended townsfolk. Instead, he connected in a new way with the poor and with his neighbors. His renewed connection with his fellow humans arose from his connection with Jesus and then in turn deepened that very connection.

A spiritual practice is thus not a self-care program, a strategy for reducing stress, or a relaxation technique. That's not to say that a life shaped by spiritual practices cannot result in a healthier soul or a sense of tranquility. But pursuing any of these ends for their own sake puts all the focus on you. Spiritual practices, by contrast, connect us to something, to someone, beyond ourselves. That connection is the point. We don't seek this connection in order to get something out of it, something we value more than the connection itself. Paradoxically, that is how we become most truly ourselves. So perhaps it will make sense to you when I say that worship is the spiritual practice upon which all other practices are grounded and from which all other practices emerge. It is through worship, you see, that God knits us together as the body of Christ. In my Episcopal tradition we worship with Word and sacrament—with Holy Scripture and Holy Meal—each Sunday. Let's turn first to the latter.

## Sharing Holy Communion

In the Last Supper Jesus instituted the Holy Eucharist or Holy Communion. Jesus took bread, gave thanks, and broke the bread.

Then he said, "This is my body, which is given for you. Do this in remembrance of me" (Luke 22:19). Christians have argued about the meaning of these words for centuries. Some have insisted that the essence of the bread itself is transformed into the body of Christ. Others say that it remains bread, but Jesus is also in the bread somehow. Still others insist that Jesus simply instituted a memorial meal using bread. In my own Episcopal tradition, we sidestep all of this. Or maybe we combine all of it. Anyway, we say that Jesus is truly present when we gather for worship. We use the phrase Real Presence. In the practice of hearing the Word and receiving the sacrament we are re-membering, knitting together again, the body of Christ. We are connected to Jesus and connected to one another through Jesus. In worship we become what we truly are: the body of Christ. And none of us can be the body of Christ—none of us can enjoy a full-hearted life—all on our own. We do it together. Writing about Holy Communion, Nora Gallagher says, "More than any other practice, taking Communion forces us to be with others, to stand with them in a circle or kneel at the altar rail or pass a tray of grape juice and cubes of bread. We are forced to be with strangers and people we don't like, persons of different colors and those with bad breath or breathing cheap alcohol. . . . It forces 'them' to be with 'us' and us to be with them."[54] Through the act of worship we practice what the Ubuntu philosophy says: "I am because we are." We see ourselves by genuinely seeing the Other.

We know that Jesus taught us to respect the dignity of every human being. And of course, that's because God loves each and every one of us. But it is also because each of us needs to discover ourselves as the beloved. That's not a truth that anybody else can just tell us. We have to have our own I-feel-seen moments. Only another somebody can see you. If we look at everybody around us as a nobody, then there's nobody there to see us. In what may seem like a paradox, we most fully recognize ourselves as the Beloved

---

54. Gallagher, *The Sacred Meal*, 12.

when we love others. That's the point of the parable of Lazarus and the rich man.

You may be accustomed to referring to this story as the parable of Lazarus and Dives. But that's a misleading title. "Dives" just means "rich" in Latin. The fellow doesn't actually have a name, and that turns out to be a crucial detail (Luke 16:19-31). To see what I mean, let's turn to the parable. It goes like this. A rich man wore designer clothes and lived on a palatial estate. He ate like a king at every meal. Lazarus—homeless, starving, and covered with sores— huddled outside the rich guy's gate. The implication is that the rich man ignored Lazarus's suffering entirely. His attention was fixed on his own comfort and pleasure. Lazarus, as far as the rich man was concerned, didn't even exist. He was a nobody. The parable's setting then shifts to the afterlife. Lazarus goes to heaven. The rich man lands in hell. Crucially, Lazarus has a name in the hereafter. The rich man remains the nameless guy. In the afterlife, we get a God's-eye view of things. On earth, Lazarus had no possessions, no status, no power. None of that stuff matters. He is God's Beloved because, well, God. And Lazarus realizes it.

The rich guy is nameless. He does not and cannot see himself as God's Beloved. That's because he has never learned to recognize anyone else as God's Beloved. He's loved things. And strictly speaking, loving things as things is fine. But he's never loved people as people; as vulnerable, tender, fragile beings who need love and offer love. God sees us all. Not with eyes of judgment and wrath. But with eyes of love. We all need, we all yearn, to say "I feel seen." And that's why Jesus told us to love one another as he loves us. That sort of love doesn't come automatically. It's a habit we hone over time, with practice. We practice it when we gather around the holy table. In addition to the Holy Table, regular worship involves being transformed by hearing the Holy Scripture read aloud and preached. We'll turn now to how hearing the Word shapes our everyday life into the way of love.

## Hearing the Word

In worship, we hear the Word read aloud and preached by fellow believers. Regular old human beings may be speaking, but our intention is to listen for and to internalize the teachings of Jesus. To hear Jesus himself speaking to us about how to walk the way of love. Think of practicing the way of love in everyday life as analogous to playing a musical instrument. Hearing the Word is like the process of learning to play that instrument by ear. In worship services we repeatedly observe how a master does it, and then we try to emulate his style and technique in our daily comings and goings.

Let's take as an analogy the great Delta blues musician Robert Johnson (1911–38). When he first hit the juke joint scene, he was a middling guitarist, and was nothing special. He made the rounds of the Mississippi Delta for a short while, then he dropped out of sight. Six months later he returned. His skills had skyrocketed. To give you some idea of what he sounded like when he reappeared, here's what the famous Rolling Stones guitarist Keith Richards reportedly said when he first heard one of Johnson's recordings: "Who's that other guy he's playing with?" There was no other guy. Johnson was playing solo. His style was so complex and so advanced that it sounded like two people playing simultaneously. Because Johnson's abilities had improved that much in such a short span of time, the legend arose that he had sold his soul to the devil to get them. But fellow bluesman Johnny Sines insisted that Johnson himself never said such a thing.[55] Instead, as music historians speculate, Johnson probably learned by listening to the radio and to records; by listening to musicians who awed him with their technique and moved him with their tone. He wanted to play like those artists. And so he listened. He internalized what he heard, and he brought those influences to new life in his own

---

55. See the documentary *Remastered: Devil at the Crossroads* on Netflix. Read also Reggie Ugwu, "Overlooked No More: Robert Johnson, Bluesman Whose Life Was a Riddle," *The New York Times*, October 21, 2019, https://www.nytimes.com/2019/09/25/obituaries/robert-johnson-overlooked.html.

fingers. His style was more than mere mimicry. It was a new cre-ation. *He* was a new creation because he had attentively listened to his teachers; he really heard them and honored them by making their lessons his own.

And by analogy that is what we do when we listen to the Word at worship: we strain to hear Jesus's teaching. Really hear it. So that we will make it our own. We listen to the Word read aloud and proclaimed in the pulpit because it shapes us. It transforms us into who we were created to be from the beginning. That's one of the lessons of the peculiar story that we call the Transfiguration. It goes like this. Jesus went to the top of a mountain, bringing with him Peter, James, and John. While they were there, Jesus was transfigured. To paraphrase Matthew, his face blazed like the sun and his clothes shimmered like snow on a cloudless day. In other words, they saw him for who he really is: love in the flesh, secure in being God's beloved and unhesitatingly loving. Love poured down into him from God and poured out to others from within him. The Beloved and the Lover (Matthew 17:1-8; Mark 9:2-8; Luke 9:28-36).

And in that moment, they glimpsed who they had always yearned to be without quite realizing it. Their true selves. The image of God. It's who we want to be. We want to know how to love like this guy does. A heavenly voice told them, and tells us, how to go about getting that desire met. It said, "Listen to him!" (Matthew 17:5). Hearing the Word is a crucial part of how we learn to love. Like I said above, loving is sort of like playing the guitar. You're not going to be very good at it initially. You might stink it up for a while. To get really good at it, you will need a trustworthy mentor. Under your mentor's guidance, you'll eventually be banging out a recogniz-able tune. In time, a few of us will become virtuosos. Most of us will play imperfectly. And while everyone's style will be recognizably their own, those who know how to listen will recognize within each of those styles the same mentor's influence. That's why it's OK for us to keep playing even though we do so imperfectly. It's also why confession is an important part of worship.

## Progress Not Perfection

Worship nourishes us and emboldens us to go into the world to love in the name of Christ. Most of us will do our best. Few of us, if any, will be flawless in the attempt. That's why confession is part of worship in my tradition. But it's important to understand that the content of confession does not boil down to this: I'm bad because I'm not perfect. Instead, I think it's better to summarize the theme of confession something like this: God, I haven't loved you or my neighbor with my whole heart, and I want—I need—your help to do that. One of my old teachers was getting at this idea when he told us a story about himself. He said, "I used to be perfect, and I was miserable. So I went to therapy. Now I'm all screwed up, but I'm really happy." It can be terribly difficult to admit when we're wrong. That our choices and our actions have taken us deep into the weeds. At some level we sense that coming clean about our blunders and missteps offers the only way out of the mess we're in. But man, it's hard. It's emotionally risky.

Psychologists tell us that when we struggle to admit that we're wrong it's because of what they call cognitive dissonance. If the world presents us with evidence that contradicts our beliefs, we're likely to experience an inner tension. Our turmoil becomes especially acute when the world tells us that we're wrong about who we think we are. That's exactly what John the Baptist was telling the people around Jerusalem: "You're not all that. You really need to admit it. Like, you know, now." Or as Matthew's Gospel puts it, "Repent, for the kingdom of heaven has come near" (Matthew 3:2). You might have heard John's words as something like this. God is coming soon. You do not measure up. At all. God has high standards. And even if God grades on a curve, you're not going to make the cut. Get your act together before it's too late. As for me, I hear something different. It goes like this: You're only as sick as your secrets. Keeping those secrets about your messy old self is exactly what makes you sick. Your problem is that you assume that you have to make yourself lovable.

Look, God isn't just on the way to you from a distant planet. God is here. Right now. Already deeply involved in your life. God knows everything, simply everything, about you. And God loves you to death. Sort of literally. You're already God's Beloved. Life is not about making yourself worth loving. Life is about discovering and then acting like you are the Beloved. Paradoxically, we discover the depth to which we are loved precisely when we admit our messiness. We are loved because, well, Jesus. Not because of us. Not because of what we accomplish or achieve. That's just who Jesus is. And here's the deal. Not only does knowing that God loves us give us the courage and the freedom to admit just how messy we can be. That admission carries us a step toward the full-hearted life we seek. A beloved person can forgive, even themselves. A beloved person begins to heal and offers compassion to the wounded. A beloved person responds to another's need without weighing what they might deserve.

Now don't get me wrong. Like my old teacher said, you and I have quite a way to go. From time to time, we will hurt other people, get resentful or envious, struggle to be generous or forgive, say things (at least in our heads) that make Jesus run for the airsickness bag. John the Baptist told his listeners that he baptized with water to mark their repentance. He wasn't announcing their graduation from human boneheadedness. No, that involves another. Another would come to baptize with the Spirit and with fire. That other of course is Jesus. The presence of Jesus in our lives is like fire. Not the destructive fire that blisters skin and razes villages. His is the fire that warms and transforms. Patiently. Often imperceptibly. Over time. So, in our worship, we admit to God and to one another that we're not perfect. That we need help. And that's what spiritual progress looks like.

# Spiritual Reflections and Exercises

1. Take a look at your schedule over the last month. To what activities have you devoted the greatest amount of time? Have those activities made your life seem more meaningful, added value to your life, and given you a sense of purpose? If you are a follower of Jesus or would like to try it on for size, give these exercises a go. Seek to devote these ordinary practices to God. For the next week or so, begin your day prayerfully devoting all your usual routines to God's loving purposes. Ask God to use your work, your childcare, your household chores, your leisure as instruments of grace, healing, and reconciliation.

2. Does the idea of functional atheism ring true to you? Have you seen it in yourself? To move beyond it, set aside a regular time to meditate on something that conveys what God's love has done and is doing for you. That could be an image of the cross, the empty tomb, the manger.

3. If regular worship attendance feeds your soul, discuss what it is about worship that does this. And if you're not nurtured by worship, talk about what does or would nurture your soul.

4. Do you sense that you are growing spiritually? If so, share what has been nurturing that growth. If not, what would you find helpful?

5. Have you ever prayed or considered praying? Do you have a regular pattern of prayers? Has God ever responded to your prayers? Give some examples. Have you ever heard God speaking to you? Tell a story about that.

*Prayer*: Ever-loving God, you give yourself to us before we even ask. We long for you even when we do not realize it. Help me to recognize that union with you is my deepest longing. And guide me in my daily comings and goings, so that all that I do is a response to the love that you have already given me. In the name of your Son, Jesus. Amen.

*Spiritual formation prepares us for a life in which*
*we move away from our fears, compulsions, resentments,*
*and sorrows, to serve with joy and courage in the world,*
*even when this leads us to places we would rather not go.*

—Henri J. M. Nouwen,
*Spiritual Formation: Following the Movements of the Spirit*

Chapter Seven

# From Wellness to Well-Being

OUR YOUNG FRIEND H. WORKS long hours, often getting to work well before dawn. At the end of the day, she takes the edge off with a long soak in a warm, fragrant tub accompanied by calming tones streaming from a smartphone app. It would come as a surprise to her if I suggested that she was practicing self-care. In fact, I'm pretty sure she would say, "Nope. Just chillin'." Still, her bath oil purchases are helping to fuel the vastly lucrative wellness industry. Consumers spend billions of dollars on self-care products: oils, supplements, lotions, diets, relaxation techniques, and fitness programs. And no wonder. The pace, the pressures, and the uncertainties of modern life leave many of us feeling harried, anxious, and exhausted. Plenty of us would welcome a little relief. And when it comes to giving us a temporary break from the stresses and the strains of life as usual, self-care products can be helpful. But the wellness industry's financial success lies in more than an offer of short-lived relief. They tap into a deeper longing than our desire to have one good night's sleep or to be rid of the bags under our aging eyes. The industry thrives on the fact that we all want to be at peace with the life that we are actually living. To be at home in our own skin and in harmony with the people around us. To sense that we're up to the next challenge and that, all things considered, we've been doing this life thing pretty well. As it turns out, the ideal of the full-hearted life encompasses all of these things. It involves our enduring character, not merely experiences of temporary relief or relaxation. And so, as I explain below, what I mean by the full-hearted life has much in common with what philosophers and theologians have called well-being.

As the psychiatrist and author Pooja Lakshmin points out, the wellness industry treats the surface of our lives. She noticed that her own patients enjoy only fleeting results from the use of their products. After applying lotions, lighting scented candles, and using mindfulness apps, her clients frequently return to their previous levels of stress and insecurity. She argues that we need to deepen the idea of wellness. In her view, true wellness requires that we look within at our own core values. She defines true wellness as aligning our lives with the values we discover within the depths of our psyche.[56] The concept of the well-being also involves aligning our lives with our foundational values. However, Lakshmin's approach remains within the bounds of secular consciousness. For her, values reside within our individual consciousness. We must look within to find them. Christians, by contrast, seek to align ourselves with a transcendent source of value. Instead of relying solely on psychological analysis to live an authentic life, we open ourselves to a relationship with a person beyond ourselves. Jesus is that person. And in him we experience a friend, a mentor, and a guide who shows us how to navigate the world as the beloved children of God. He shows us how to live well, how to forgive, how to channel our

---

56. Pooja Lakshmin, *Real Self-Care* (New York: Penguin Random House, 2023); see or listen to Ezra Klein's interview with the author, "Boundaries, Burnout, and the 'Goopification' of Self-Care," *The New York Times*, September 19, 2023, https://www.nytimes.com/2023/09/19/opinion/ezra-klein-podcast-pooja-lakshmin.html.

anger, and how to be courageous. Christians call a life shaped by these practices *well-being*. In what follows we'll get to each of these practices in turn. But first, let's look more closely at the difference between wellness and well-being.

## Wellness and Well-Being

As I mentioned above, the wellness industry operates within the confines of secular consciousness. That is to say, all meaning, purpose, and value are subjective. We can observe objective reality with our senses. We can weigh it, measure it, and agree upon its contours as a result. Values, by contrast, do not exist in that objective world. They reside in the private consciousness—in the heart and mind—of each individual. Your values and my values may happen to agree. But there is nothing out there beyond us that either justifies or invalidates what we prefer or what we hold dear as individual subjects. Accordingly, aligning my life with my values amounts to inhabiting a pattern of life that expresses my deeply held dreams and priorities. So even when our pursuit of wellness goes deep in the way that Lakshmin suggests that it should, it remains a function of self-expression and self-fulfillment.

Jesus certainly stresses sincerity, and nothing quite gets his ire up like religious hypocrisy. However, he consistently presses for more than staying true to your own private set of values. His parables are littered with contemplative challenges to the soundness of the values that guide us. Are those values worth holding? Will they sustain us when the chips are down? For instance, the wise build their houses on rock. Fools choose sand. Which are you, wise or foolish (Matthew 7:24-27)? Give all you have to purchase the pearl of great price. Are you devoting your life to something really worth the cost (Matthew 13:45-46)? Jesus teaches us to do the hard, honest, and courageous work of aligning our values with a higher standard; to align them with the divine care for all things rather than the narrow standard of self-expression and self-fulfillment.

Jesus teaches us that God wove a moral order into the fabric of the universe. This is not to say that God merely gave us a set of rules to follow robotically. God did not give Moses the Ten Commandments to make us into rigid, unreflective rule followers. Instead, those ten laws, and the Hebrew Bible's moral directives about individual conduct and social order in general, are examples of what a caring life could look like in various circumstances. That's why Jesus summarized the law as the law of love. Love God with every fiber of your being. Love your neighbor like the quality of your own life cannot be separated from theirs. In other words, even when it includes deep psychological work, the concept of wellness remains bound to each individual's value system. Jesus is certainly concerned about each of us individually. But well-being involves aligning our habitual practices with a moral order that transcends our private, inner life.

To put this in slightly different terms, consider how philosophers and theologians have thought about happiness. Some have said that happiness is pleasure. Conversely, unhappiness is pain, frustration, or disappointment. This school of thought has been called hedonism (derived from the Greek word for pleasure, *hedonia*). Mind you, hedonism is not necessarily the heedless, self-centered pursuit of physical gratification. For instance, the moral theory called utilitarianism champions the greatest happiness principle. The good is what promotes the highest level of pleasure for the greatest number of people. And this includes intellectual and cultural pleasures of the mind, heart, and soul. But there's a problem with every form of hedonism. Nothing is inherently valuable. The value of any human life is measured by a hedonistic calculus. If the greatest good for the greatest number can be achieved through the suffering of a minority, then it would be morally justifiable for us to pursue such a course. What passes for the common good is only the greatest pleasure for the largest possible majority.

In contrast to hedonism, there is a tradition that defines happiness as becoming the fully human person we were created to be. The Greek word that this school of thought used for happiness is *eudaimonia*. Strictly speaking, that word is better translated as "well-being," or even "being well." Achieving excellence at being a person. Moral philosophers and theologians call that kind of excellence virtue, and they describe an array of virtuous behaviors to which we should all aspire. I won't go into detail about them here, but it is crucial to note that a virtuous life cannot be separated from the idea of pursuing the common good. Wisdom, for instance, is excellence at navigating life in community. A courageous person faces danger to preserve the common good. And tellingly, the philosopher Aristotle named friendship—the bond of affection at the very foundation of all authentic communities—as one of the chief virtues.

That's what a full-hearted life looks like. We live for the sake of the love that we give one another. Even under dreary circumstances—and especially in hard and perilous times—loving one another makes life meaningful. As it turns out, Jesus taught us how to be happy: love your neighbor as yourself. Loving our neighbor doesn't make us happy because of what our neighbor does or says in response to our love. Happiness comes along with loving our neighbor because that's just who we are at our very core. We are always free to love. No one can rob us of that freedom. And we can see this most clearly in the practice of forgiveness.

## Practicing Forgiveness

On August 27, 2020, Hurricane Laura made landfall in Southwest Louisiana with winds of nearly 150 miles per hour. Laura's winds still exceeded 100 miles per hour as it passed through our home in Central Louisiana. At dusk the following day, my wife, Joy, our daughter Meredith, our dog Gracie, and I were strolling through our battered neighborhood. Shattered trees, broken branches, and all manner of debris lined either side of the street. People had begun the hard, long, and tedious work of restoring their homes and their yards to some semblance of pre-storm normal. Looking around, I had what may seem an odd moment of clarity: "I always knew that my mother loved me, no matter what. But I had to keep trying to prove myself to my father to win his love, to make a connection, and I never succeeded." If you're one of my regular readers, you might be thinking, "Well, no kidding!" As I've discussed elsewhere, my father was emotionally and physically abusive, so much so that my mother fled with me carrying not much more with us than the clothes on our backs.[57]

Maybe the sight of heap after heap of things so broken that they could only be discarded crystallized my thinking about the shattered thing that was our relationship. Those heaps stood as visual metaphors for one of my chief spiritual challenges: to forgive where genuine reconciliation wasn't likely to happen. Unless you snooze your way through the Gospels, you can't avoid noticing that Jesus teaches his followers to forgive and to seek reconciliation. Forgiveness is a one-way street. You and I can forgive no matter what. It's not always easy to do. For that matter, forgiving another person for a serious injury can be a lifelong process. But Jesus teaches us to forgive whether or not the other person is sorry for what they did. He told us to turn the other cheek; to love our enemy.

Forgiveness is for our own good, really. As Anne Lamott likes to say, refusing to forgive is like drinking rat poison and waiting for the rat to die.[58] It kills you from the inside and does not the first bit of harm to the one you want to get back at. What Lamott says is true enough. But in addition to that, we shape the world every time we act. When we forgive, we cast our vote for a world where broken things get mended. When we retaliate, we've chosen to make a more fractured, less habitable planet for everybody,

---

57. See Owensby, *A Resurrection Shaped Life*, 4–6.
58. Anne Lamott, *Traveling Mercies: Some Thoughts on Faith* (New York: Anchor Books, 1999), 134.

ourselves included. Forgiveness opens the way to reconciliation, to the restoration of a fractured relationship. But unlike forgiveness, reconciliation is a two-way street. Here's how I have put it elsewhere: "Reconciliation is always reciprocal. The injured person's forgiveness is met with genuine remorse and amended behavior. While the relationship will probably not return to what it was like before it was broken, a new kind of relationship can gradually emerge."[59]

The challenge I faced with my father was to forgive him even though I never heard him apologize and sensed no fundamental change in his character. Honestly, I can't claim perfection on the whole forgiveness thing, but I've made some progress. I say that I've made progress on the basis of Jesus's teaching about frayed and tattered relationships. In Matthew's Gospel, Jesus outlines a process for holding a sinner accountable and seeking reconciliation. It seems to have been originally a teaching about congregations as a whole, but it applies to personal relationships as well. First you talk to the one who injured you. If that person just won't listen, you invite others from your shared circle of friends to join in the process. Finally, if the offending person simply refuses to admit wrongdoing and change their ways, you have to admit that reconciliation is not going to happen anytime soon. At that point, you relate to the person "as a gentile and a tax collector" (Matthew 18:17). Some have read this text as permission to shun others or to excommunicate them. But since Jesus explicitly befriended Gentiles and tax collectors, I draw a different conclusion. Turning again to what I've written elsewhere, "When we forgive an unrepentant person, forgiveness takes the form of reinforced boundaries and keeping a safe distance."[60] The relationship may be strained and may cause serious heartache, but forgiveness leaves open the possibility of reconciliation in the future. You never simply discard another person. My father died in 2006. We were still estranged. But I have not lost hope in a future

59. Owensby, *A Resurrection Shaped Life*, 69.
60. Owensby, *A Resurrection Shaped Life*, 68.

reconciliation. After all, reconciliation is ultimately God's work. The work of infinite love. A love that mends all things. Even if it takes eternity.

So, as a preliminary step in learning to be a forgiving person, Jesus tells us to do this: "When you are offering your gift at the altar, if you remember that your brother or sister has something against you, leave your gift there before the altar and go; first be reconciled to your brother or sister, and then come and offer your gift" (Matthew 5:23-24). In other words, start learning how to forgive by remembering that you've hurt somebody. You've probably heard that hurt people hurt people. That seems true to me. Jesus appears to have thought so too. But he wants us to draw a different, deeper lesson from that saying than what we normally derive. Well-meaning friends and pastors and teachers have probably told you to remember that the person who has hurt you was probably hurt by someone else. That's how they're dealing with their own pain. The idea is that you'll be more likely to forgive the offender because you understand this about them.

Jesus turns this sideways. He says, yes, hurt people hurt people. And you're a hurt person. So that probably means that you've hurt people. Jesus edges us away from focusing on the injury someone else has caused us to the pain that we have caused others. He helps us get over ourselves. Paradoxically, we discover that we are already forgiven only once we realize that we need it. It may seem odd, but contrition—our sincere remorse for hurting somebody else—is a kind of knowing: knowing that God loves us; knowing our true self as the beloved. And that's the first step to being a habitual forgiver. In the end, we don't forgive because Jesus tells us that we have to do so or that God will forgive us only once we do. We forgive because we realize that we are forgiven. In other words, at least for a moment, we extend the love that has been and is being perpetually poured out upon us. Recognizing ourselves as God's beloved is also the key to the next practice: channeling our anger.

## Channeling Our Anger

As if we didn't already know this, polls tell us that a lot of people are angry these days.[61] Habitual, stuck on steady-boil angry. We're not talking about a measured righteous indignation at injustice or the momentary blood pressure spikes at life's little indignities and frustrations. No, the research reveals a persistent, irritable resentment. If, like me, you're an intuitive person, you have probably sensed other people's anger as you waited to check out at the grocery store, stood in line at the post office, commuted to work on a jammed freeway, or felt jostled by a large crowd of strangers making their way through a narrow exit at a stadium. It's an aggression just under some other person's skin. If you've spent any sustained time around this kind of simmering anger—maybe in the family or at work—you know what it's like to have to walk on eggshells or to be constantly prepared for a fight. And honestly, if you're like me, you might know all too well what it's like to wrestle with anger rising up within yourself.

The anger infecting our common life does more than unsettle our inner lives. It erodes the bonds that hold us together as a society. If we want a world worth living in, we're going to have to do something about it. And I believe that Jesus shows us the basic

---

61. See Amina Dunn, "Most Voters Are 'Fearful' and 'Angry' About the State of the U.S., but a Majority Now are 'Hopeful,' Too," Pew Research Center, November 20, 2020, https://www.pewresearch.org/short-reads/2020/11/20/most-voters-are-fearful-and-angry-about-the-state-of-the-u-s-but-a-majority-now-are-hopeful-too/; Carrie Dann, "A Deep and Boiling Anger: NBC/WSJ Poll Finds a Pessimistic America Despite Current Economic Satisfaction," NBC News, August 25, 2019, https://www.nbcnews.com/politics/meet-the-press/deep-boiling-anger-nbc-wsj-poll-finds-pessimistic-america-despite-n1045916; Julie Ray, "Americans' Stress, Worry and Anger Intensified in 2018," Gallup, April 25, 2019, https://news.gallup.com/poll/249098/americans-stress-worry-anger-intensified-2018.aspx; Scott Hensley, "Poll: Americans Say We're Angrier Than a Generation Ago," June 26, 2019, NPR, https://www.npr.org/sections/health-shots/2019/06/26/735757156/poll-americans-say-were-angrier-than-a-generation-ago.

principle for getting a grip on our own anger and for dealing with other people's projectile grumpiness. Jesus starts with a posture of solidarity and compassion. He's one of us. So he knows in his marrow that people are going to be, well, people. And that's a good, if sometimes trying, thing. To borrow the title from one of Kate Bowler's books, there's no cure for being human.[62] In this context, what I'm saying is that Jesus is clear that people are going to get angry. Each of us will feel our blood boil at some point. And odds are better than even that we'll all be on the receiving end of somebody else's temper eventually.

But contrary to what you may have heard, Jesus did not devise a "Just Say No" campaign for stamping out anger once and for all. Anger, you see, is not a sin to be avoided. It's a human emotion. What is good or bad, virtuous or sinful about anger comes down to how we navigate it. Not that we feel it. Neuropsychologists tell us that anger is a natural and even necessary emotion. It starts in our sympathetic, that is to say, in our *involuntary* nervous system. When faced with a perceived threat we automatically go into the fight-flight-freeze mode in order to survive. Like I said, it's a human thing.

Gregory the Great (c. 540–604) famously listed seven root vices that give rise to all the immoral behavior on this planet. You may have heard that he put anger on that list. But actually, Gregory's original Latin for this sin should be rendered as "wrath," or even better, as "rage." He has in mind what happens when normal, natural anger spins out of control. To get his point, consider that "rage" and "rabies" share the same linguistic roots. On analogy with rabies, rage is like a deadly and contagious disease. Powerful emotions sweep away a person that we have known and leaves in their place an impulsively aggressive, potentially violent creature. And perhaps worse, wrath's bite passes along the illness to its victims. Rage can produce rage in others. So, being human and all, Jesus faced exactly the same challenge we do on an everyday basis: dealing with

---

62. Kate Bowler, *There No Cure for Being Human: And Other Truths I Need to Hear* (New York: Random House, 2021).

our own anger in a healthy way and responding constructively to the angry people who cross our path. And whether he's handling his own inner stuff or navigating the turbulence of other people's fury, Jesus draws on one basic principle: Remember who you are and what your life is about. One of Jesus's early conflict stories illustrates what I mean.

Jesus preached in his hometown synagogue. His neighbors were thrilled. At least, that was their initial reaction. But in an instant, the crowd turned violently against him. As Luke put it, "All in the synagogue were filled with rage. They got up, drove him out of the town, and led him to the brow of the hill on which their town was built, so that they might hurl him off the cliff" (Luke 4:28-29). What set them off was Jesus's core message: God's love is for everybody. No exceptions. Nobody's religion or moral rectitude or country of origin gives them an inside track. God loves because God loves. In response to their violent rage, Jesus "passed through the midst of them and went on his way" (Luke 4:30). In other words, he embodied his principle for engaging an enraged, hurting, confused, oppressed, perilous world. He went on his way. *His* way. He remembered who he was and what his life was all about (see Luke 4:21-30).

At his baptism in the Jordan, Jesus had heard who he truly is: the beloved (Mark 1:4-11). And the only way to be true to that identity is to love. And so, no matter what the world dished out, Jesus responded as the beloved. As the one who loves what God loves how God loves it. By loving, Jesus refused—and we can refuse—to amplify and spread the rage that shatters hearts and breaks bodies. Instead, our love acts as leaven, as that small, often imperceptible element that prevents the mass of dough from simply collapsing in on itself; that prevents coercion and violence from being the defining word for all things human. Channeling our own anger and healing a world infected by rage begins with remembering who we are and what our life is all about. We are the beloved. And love is what we are all about. Let's remember who we are. And let's be courageous enough to live into it.

Courage

To speak normally—to make intelligible sounds that other people could understand—I had to undergo two lengthy surgeries. The first happened when I was just a toddler. There's not much I can tell you about that one. I have no memory of it at all. The second time around I was in my early twenties. For six hours a surgeon harvested tissue from my throat and from the sides of my mouth. Using those strips of flesh, he built what is called a pharyngeal flap. To make a long anatomical story short, he gave me the soft palate (the roof of my mouth) that nature had neglected to provide for me at birth. Following that procedure, I remained on a liquid diet for a couple of months. There are tons of lessons that growing up with a speech impediment and that undergoing major surgeries taught me. But none of them is more important than this one: I've got a body. And to be embodied is to suffer. So taking life on its own terms and making sense of it involves learning how to navigate suffering. In other words, a life worth living requires courage. And, in its truest sense, courage is an expression of love.

Hollywood's depiction of courage tends to be narrowly focused on physical risk-taking. Tough characters—male and female alike—face bodily harm and near-certain death. Scripts tend to portray them as fearless. And that should be your first clue that Hollywood doesn't know much about courage. True courage isn't the absence of fear. Various psychologists and philosophers have defined courage as the ability to confront our fears and to do what needs to be done. Aristotle insisted that bravery requires wisdom. Courageous people know what is worthy of fear in specific situations and what isn't. They respond appropriately to dangers and challenges on the basis of who they are and what those particular circumstances call for. Moreover, wise people not only overcome their fears, they know *why* they should face them. Reflecting on the life of Jesus has led me to think that, while Aristotle is right, his thoughts on courage are missing a crucial element: *What* we fear is suffering. It may be physical pain or emotional anguish, the sting of rejection or the crushing weight of grief, a disfiguring injury or a broken heart. But in the end, it's suffering that makes us tremble or hesitate, flee or fly into a rage.

We can't completely avoid suffering. So our aim as humans is to make something good and beautiful and meaningful from a life that inevitably involves bruises to body and soul. I regret to say that, left to our own devices, we humans all too often make a wreck of things. We hurt and we're afraid of being hurt. So we hurt others in response to being injured and we preemptively attack others to protect ourselves. I'm thinking of every war and feud and violent crime in history. Every act of retaliation ranging from petty passive aggressiveness to capital punishment. As I said above, hurt people hurt people. And we're all hurt people. So we're stuck on a hamster wheel of suffering.

Jesus is working—through the likes of you and me—to get us off that hamster wheel. He sends his disciples into the world to "cure the sick, raise the dead, cleanse those with skin disease, cast out demons" (Matthew 10:8), to restore fractured bodies and souls, to transform this bruising world into a beloved community. Jesus and his followers are on a peace mission. In the Sermon on the Mount, he assured us that peacemakers are blessed. They would be called the children of God. And so, it is jarring to hear him say, "Do not think that I have come to bring peace to the earth; I have not come to bring peace but a sword" (Matthew 10:34).

As it turns out, plenty of people will perceive peacemakers as troublemakers, as bearing a sword. That's because making peace begins with identifying and dismantling the toxic, dehumanizing, destructive patterns in our individual lives and in our common lives. The late congressman and civil rights leader John Lewis called this good trouble. And he knew from personal experience that good trouble can be met with violent resistance, with beatings and incarceration, and with suffering. Jesus himself was clear about it. He understood that his path would lead to the cross and that his followers should be prepared for persecution. That's why he told us, "Do not fear those who kill the body but cannot kill the soul" (Matthew 10:28).

In other words, be brave. Make good trouble even and especially when it makes your gut churn. Let love animate you in the face of hate and violence. That's how Jesus went to the cross. He

responded to human violence with love. He understood that love—
and only love—can make something good and beautiful and meaningful from suffering. Only love can bring greater life from misery.
You see, that's what God is about in Jesus from the very start. When
God chose to be embodied, God knew that suffering would come
along with the deal. To be human at all—to have flesh—is to suffer.
And in Jesus, God shows us that love transforms suffering. The cross
leads to the empty tomb. To a whole new kind of life. To mend this
aching world will take courage. And Jesus teaches us that real courage is an expression of love.

## Spiritual Reflections and Exercises

1. Can you be happy in the midst of hard times? If so, talk
   about how you understand happiness. What would be the
   source of that happiness?

2. Have life experiences ever led you to reexamine your values?
   Was God in that for you? If so, where?

3. Talk about a time that you needed and received forgiveness
   and a time that you have forgiven another person. What
   was difficult? Did the experience change you? If so, talk
   about how.

4. Discuss anger using these questions as a guide. How do
   you respond to another person's anger? Is it hard for you to
   express anger? Has your anger ever gotten the best of you?
   How do you express your own anger in a healthy way? What
   sorts of things genuinely call for anger? Has your anger ever
   been misplaced? When might anger be a virtue? A vice?

5. What do you think of first when you hear the word *courage*? Do think that Jesus was courageous in the garden of
   Gethsemane? What sort of courage was that?

6. Talk about a time that you showed moral or spiritual courage. What helped you to be brave?

*Prayer*: Holy God, you have created us in your image. Help us to love as your son Jesus taught us to love. Give us the grace to forgive as we are forgiven and the courage to do the right thing when the cost is high. In Jesus's name. Amen.

*Our goal is to create a beloved community
and this will require a qualitative change in our souls
as well as a quantitative change in our lives.*

—Martin Luther King,
"Nonviolence: The Only Road to Freedom"

Chapter Eight

# Justice and the Full-Hearted Community

OUR DAUGHTER IS NEURODIVERGENT. When she was seven, a psychologist told us that her way of processing things falls within the autism spectrum. Bright and perpetually cheerful, Meredith has a quirky sense of humor, and her contributions to conversations can come from an unusual perspective. Like most of us, Meredith wants to be herself and she wants to belong to a community in a meaningful way. But picking up on social cues did not come naturally to her. So, aware that she faced a challenge, Meredith intentionally learned to recognize common neurotypical social cues in order to make connections with others. Her colleagues at work and the members of her church choir enjoy her company and appreciate her skills. Mostly, they're neurotypicals. And they've provided the kind of interpersonal on-ramp that allows Meredith to belong and to be herself. I tell you all of this to illustrate that a full-hearted community takes work, commitment, compassion, respect, and understanding for both the individual and the group. Or, as Cornel West likes to say, "Justice is what love looks like in public."[63]

Jesus taught us to love our neighbor as ourselves; to care as much about their life as we care about our own. Love is more than how I happen to feel about somebody or how they feel about me. It is the creative, redeeming, reconciling power of God at work in and through each of us. Divine love flows through the good that we can do in each moment for our neighbors near and far, no matter how insignificant that good may seem. Even the smallest act of mercy is an expression of the divine love. When the prophet Amos said, "Let justice roll down like waters" (Amos 5:24), he was urging us toward a society that embodies this sort of love. A social order like this remains an aspiration. A dream. But it is God's dream. Clearly, I'm not claiming that if we would simply adjust our attitudes justice would instantly appear. There is much hard work to do in our common and in our interior life. This takes time and effort. But we can trust in two things. First, God plays the long game. There may be no magic wand that instantly fixes personal and social ills, but God is relentlessly, if sometime inscrutably, edging us on toward a full-hearted community. Second, God weaves all of our small, seemingly inconsequential acts of kindness, peacemaking, and compassion together into an infinite tapestry that we finite individuals cannot see clearly. But we can dream. And that dream can guide us toward, and motivate us to strive for, a community that promotes and protects the equal dignity of every human being. The apostles themselves took this dream with them into the world.

## Divine Justice and Human Equality

The Apostle Thomas died somewhere along the southwest coast of India. According to an ancient text called The Acts

---

63. See, for instance, West's speech at Howard University from April of 2011: https://www.youtube.com/watch?v=nGqP7S_WO6o&t=21s.

of Thomas, King Misdaeus, a local ruler, blew his stack when Thomas converted his queen, his son, and his sister-in-law to the Way of Jesus. In response, Misdaeus ordered soldiers to drag Thomas outside the city to a nearby hill. There, they executed him with spears.[64] Thomas's capital offense was to introduce a religion whose precepts would undermine the established dominance hierarchy.

The term "dominance hierarchy" refers to the social structure that emerges among animals like lobsters, wolves, and chickens. Maybe you've used the phrase "pecking order." Well, that's an example of a dominance hierarchy. If you throw some feed into a chicken yard, you'll see the biggest, strongest chicken eat first. An inner circle follows next. Finally, a bedraggled, wary bunch will scurry to and fro to collect whatever remains. That last group looks, well, henpecked. Ever since they were young, these weaker chickens have been mercilessly pecked by stronger chickens whenever they approached food before everyone else was finished. These lowlier chickens avoid this torture only by remaining timid and subservient. Whenever they assert their right to the food, the beaks of the other chickens swiftly deliver pain, humiliation, and even death. In a dominance hierarchy, the strong get the most food, the most secure places to live, and the most attractive mates. Those at the top of the heap use force against anyone who threatens to unseat them from their privileged position.

The Acts of Thomas does not tell us for sure, but it does seem reasonable to suggest that Misdaeus executed Thomas because he was a threat to the hierarchy at the top of which he sat. Sure, maybe he was the kind of guy who could get murderous about differences of opinion. But it's more likely that the king's rage was triggered by changes in his subject's behavior patterns. You see,

---

64. There is a free online version of this text: "The Apocryphal New Testament," trans. and notes by M. R. James (Oxford: Clarendon Press, 1924), in The Gnostic Society Library, http://gnosis.org/library/actthom.htm. An affordable paperback translation is *The Acts of Thomas*, Harold W. Attridge and Julian V. Hills (Frederick, MD: Polebridge Press, 2010).

Thomas had established several congregations. Jesus had clearly told Thomas, "I am the way and the truth and the life" (John 14:6). Everywhere Jesus went, God got what God wanted. The sick got healthy. The blind could see. The lame began to walk. The hungry ate their fill. So when we walk the way of Jesus, God gets what God wants. God does not want the strong to get all the best stuff while everybody else gets leftovers and castoffs. God does not want a few to accumulate a garish excess while others go wanting. God wants plenty—plenty of resources, plenty of health, plenty of security—for everybody. In other words, God is not a fan of the dominance hierarchy.

We don't have to travel back in time to the ancient world to find advocates of the dominance hierarchy. Neither is it necessary to visit contemporary autocratic regimes in other parts of the globe. There are overt proponents of inequality inside the United States. Take for instance Costin Alamariu. He's the person thought to write as the controversial internet personality Bronze Age Pervert or BAP. The columnist Graeme Wood summarizes BAP's worldview this way: "[The] natural and desirable condition of life is the domination of the weak and ugly by the strong and noble."[65] BAP contends that strong individuals should strive to dominate and exploit their inferiors. That is the natural order of things in his view. The fittest thrive and survive.[66] The weak serve the strong or perish. So it is, and so it should be. The assertion that all humans are created equal is a myth used by the weak to constrain the powerful. From this perspective, it's only a short leap to the Nazi experiments in eugenics and the concentration camps aimed at purifying the human gene pool and to ensure the ascendence of a master race. It's important to remember that, from their own distorted perspective,

---

65. Graeme Wood, "How Bronze Age Pervert Charmed the Far Right," *The Atlantic*, August 3, 2023, https://www.theatlantic.com /magazine/archive/2023/09/bronze-age-pervert-costin-alamariu/674762/.

66. Interestingly, the theory of evolution defines fitness not by strength but by the ability to adapt to changing environments. But that's a topic for another day.

the Nazis were doing the right thing according to nature's own dictates. They would argue that they were simply quarantining and exterminating inferior examples of our species. In their view, the very presence of such inferior stock threatened the evolutionary advance of the human race. In fact, BAP actually writes, "I believe in rule by a military caste of men who would be able to guide society toward a morality of eugenics."[67] Even if I were not the child of a Holocaust survivor, a statement like this would make my blood run cold. It stands in sharp contrast to the vision of justice that Jesus teaches his disciples.[68]

Jesus said, "If any want to come after me, let them deny themselves and take up their cross and follow me. For those who want to save their life will lose it, and those who lose their life for my sake will find it" (Matthew 16:24-25). The way of Jesus—the way of the cross—is compassion. And compassion is more than a feeling of pity. Compassion is active solidarity. When Jesus taught us to love our neighbor as ourselves, he wasn't encouraging us to have warm and fuzzy feelings about them. He was telling us a basic truth about human existence. We are all in this together. Joined at the hip. That's why he said that whatsoever we do to the least—to the hungry, the homeless, the poor, the persecuted, the reviled, the discarded—we do to him (Matthew 25:45). A society worth living in, a society where we are all truly free, is rooted in solidarity with one another—solidarity in all our differences and struggles. A just society pursues the common good, not the good of the few at the expense of the many. The result of a world governed by compassion is the full-hearted community; a liberating, life-affirming world for all. And the principle at its center is the scriptural view that God's love makes each and every one of us infinitely valuable and worthy of unconditional respect.

_____

67. See "Communittar Fools," J'Accuse, November 25, 2021, https://www.jaccusepaper.co.uk/p/communittar-fools.

68. You can read about my mother's experience in Mauthausen Concentration Camp in my book *Looking for God in Messy Places*, pp. 41ff.

It may seem like a contradiction, but the secular approach to government—an approach that separates Church and State—is an expression of, and at its best a protection of, the Christian view of human nature. However, there are those who equate "secular" with "anti-religious" and so push for some form of Christian nationalism. As Damon Linker writes, "Those on the right primarily concerned about the fate of traditionalist Christian morals and worship in the United States insist that we already live in a regime that oppresses and brutalizes religious believers and conservatives. And they make those charges in a theologically inflected idiom that's meant to address and amplify the right's intense worries about persecution by progressives."[69] In short, proponents of Christian nationalism believe that our political system is in fact anti-Christian. Accordingly, they advocate replacing American democracy as we know it with a theocracy. Their interpretation of Christian values should become the law of the land. Depending upon who pitches the idea, Christian nationalism involves imposing patriarchal models of the family, includes more or less obvious white supremacy, and opts for religious totalitarianism over democracy.[70]

However, contrary to the fears of Christian nationalists, the secular distinction between Church and State, is not anti-religious.

---

69. Damon Linker, "Get to Know the Influential Conservative Intellectuals Who Help Explain G.O.P. Extremism," *New York Times*, November 4, 2023, https://www.nytimes.com/2023/11/04/opinion/sunday/conservative-intellectuals-republicans.html. See also Katherine Stewart, *The Power Worshippers: Inside the Dangerous Rise of Religious Nationalism* (New York: Bloomsbury Publishers, 2020); Kristin Kobes Du Mez, *Jesus and John Wayne: How Evangelicals Corrupted a Faith and Fractured a Nation* (New York: Liveright Publishing, 2020).

70. See, for example, Stephen Wolfe, *The Case for Christian Nationalism* (New York: Canon Press, 2022); Rod Dreher, *Live Not by Lies: A Manual for Christian Dissidents* (New York: Penguin Publishing Group, 2020); Patrick Deneen, *Regime Change: Toward a Postliberal Future* (New York: Swift Press, 2023).

Instead, it preserves freedom of belief by refusing to base our laws on the teachings or the texts of any specific religious organization. This is not to say that our citizens and our elected officials remain unmoved by their own moral worldviews. On the contrary, any government should pursue whatever it perceives as the good of its citizens. Moral considerations cannot be separated from the body politic. For instance, whether a member of our Congress is Christian, Jewish, Muslim, Buddhist, or atheist, they swear to uphold the Constitution, a document crafted to protect the rights of individuals. Freedom and equality are our core values as a nation. Nevertheless, we insist on a separation of Church and State. Simply put, this means that the State cannot enforce any religion's laws or impose religious doctrines upon its citizens, and each citizen is free to worship—or reject worship altogether—according to their own convictions. Every religion should be treated equally, and no one should be required to be even faintly religious. There is something deeply Jesus-y about religious tolerance. For instance, when a Samaritan village refused to follow Jesus, the disciples wanted to rain fire upon them. Jesus rebuked them (Luke 9:51-56). And of a competing exorcist Jesus once said, "Whoever is not against us is for us" (Mark 9:40).

Our secular approach to governance is always a work in progress. It's not just that we argue about the practical viability and the effectiveness of various solutions to our common challenges: national security, economic flourishing, education, crime, poverty, and the like. We must also respectfully navigate our differences about the moral imperatives that drive our decisions and the moral vision that we pursue as a society. Even though in what follows I'll be saying that justice is what God's love looks like in the public sphere, I am not suggesting that a just political system must impose explicitly Christian teachings on its citizens. However, I do argue that being a follower of Jesus means that we should advocate for policies and public practices that are consistent with the teachings of Jesus. I will say more about that in the following sections.

But at the moment, I will simply stress that the core democratic ideals of freedom and equality are derived from, or are at the very least consistent with, the Christian worldview. The idea that we should respect and guard the rights of each individual is consistent with the biblical view that human beings are inherently valuable precisely because we were created by, and created in the image of, an infinitely loving God. Everyone we meet is God's beloved. And the pursuit of a world like that gets real for us only when we face the realities of the world we actually inhabit. One of those realities is racism. And in the United States, that means coming to terms with the legacy of slavery. Among other things, this will involve reexamining the stories we have been telling ourselves about ourselves. Stories like the killings in Colfax, Louisiana, during the Reconstruction era.

## Reckoning with Racism

Before the Civil War ended, a man named Meredith Calhoun once enslaved over seven hundred people of African descent.[71] One of his massive plantations stretched across what is now the town of Colfax in Central Louisiana. Had you driven past Colfax between 1950 and 2021 you could have seen an official state historical marker memorializing the Colfax riot. The marker mischaracterized the killings of dozens of Black men and women by white men as the suppression of a riot. That marker went on to say that the courageous actions of these white men brought an "end to carpetbag misrule in the South." Lawsuits ensuing from these events resulted in Supreme Court rulings that laid the legal groundwork

---

71. The Roberson Project at The University of the South provides a wealth of information about the slave trade and many of the most prominent enslavers. See https://foundingfunders.sewanee.edu/.

for the Jim Crow era.[72] Today, a new marker stands in place of the older one. It provides a very different account of the events of April 13, 1873. That marker accurately memorializes the victims of the Colfax massacre. And perhaps just as crucially, it unearths the story that we have told ourselves about ourselves that justifies systemic racism. Let's turn first to the massacre.[73]

On April 13, 1873, Easter Sunday, around 140 heavily armed white men, led by former Confederate officers, marched on a poorly armed Black militia at the Grant Parish courthouse in Colfax. In an election the previous November, the candidates who had championed white supremacist policies had lost at the ballot box to those favoring racial equality. The attackers were bent on installing their candidates by force. A Black militia had gathered to protect the duly elected officials, both Black and white. At noon the white supremacist force began shooting at the courthouse. The defenders held their ground for two hours. In time, the white attackers opened fire with a small cannon, set fire to the courthouse, and guaranteed safety to all who gave up the fight. When the Black defenders surrendered—many waving makeshift white flags—the white mob shot them, beat them, and stabbed them. Later in that day, Black survivors were marched to a nearby field and shot in the head at close range. Estimates

---

72. The 1873 ruling in *United States v. Cruikshank* provided the context that made the *Plessy v. Ferguson* (1896) "separate but equal" ruling possible. See The Brennan Center for Justice, "It's Not About Federalism #18: The Colfax Massacre," https://www.brennancenter.org/sites/default /files/legacy/d/inaf18.pdf.

73. Faimon A. Roberts, "150 Years After White Mob Slaughtered Blacks in Rural Louisiana, New Monument Tells True Story of Colfax Massacre," April 13, 2023, https://www.nola.com/news/150-years-after -white-mob-slaughtered-blacks-in-rural-louisiana-new-monument-tells -true-story/article_a1037952-d8cc-11ed-9dfd-3726f0d0e831.html; see also Alena Noakes, "Marking History: New Memorial Unveiled on 150th Anniversary of Colfax Massacre," KALB, April 13, 2023, https://www. kalb.com/2023/04/14/marking-history-new-memorial-unveiled-150th -anniversary-colfax-massacre/.

remain imprecise, but somewhere between sixty and eighty freed-men (some sources estimate over one hundred) were murdered. A mass grave still lies under Colfax. Many of the freedmen guarding the courthouse that day had been emancipated from Meredith Calhoun's plantation.[74]

Casting the violence in Colfax as a riot rather than a massacre expressed what philosophers and sociologists call an imaginary. An imaginary is a cultural framework of meanings and values held by a group of people that reflects what the social order should properly be. It is a widely held and powerfully enforced psychosocial construct, not the reflection of objective, biological facts. Our perceptions of what is right and wrong, good and evil, just and unjust draw upon our moral or social imaginary. Our cultural, legal, and social institutions arise from, reinforce, and then perpetuate this imaginary. Kelly Brown Douglas tells us that "the moral imaginary is conspicuously shaped by the group that has been historically, culturally, and socially dominant in a nation."[75] To put it simply, an imaginary is the story we tell ourselves about ourselves. We govern our common life according to that story. We sort out who is in or out, on the top or on the bottom, as a function of that imaginary. A white supremacist imaginary tells the story of who is and who is not "white" and that "white" is a superior and hence justifiably privileged race.

The historical marker mischaracterizing those events was removed in 2021 in a ceremony at the state's direction. In attendance that day were the Rev. Avery Hamilton and Dean Woods. Hamilton is the great-great-great-grandson of Jesse McKinney, the first Black man to die in the massacre. Woods's great-great-grandfather was one of the white mob. Together Hamilton and Woods formed the Colfax

74. For a full account of the massacre and its broader historical significance, see Charles Lane, *The Day Freedom Died: The Colfax Massacre, The Supreme Court, and the Betrayal of Reconstruction* (New York: Henry Holt and Company, 2008).
75. Kelly Brown Douglas, *Resurrection Hope: A Future Where Black Lives Matter* (Maryknoll, NY: Orbis Books, 2021), 6.

Memorial Organization.[76] The group's initial aim was to produce a historically honest memorial that offered tribute to the victims. On April 13, 2023, a three-paneled black granite monument was unveiled. The left panel contains historian Charles Lane's accurate account of those events. Artist Jazzmen Lee-Johnson crafted depictions of the victims for the middle panel. On the right there is a list of the victims' names.[77]

We should celebrate the new Colfax memorial as a step in the direction of racial reconciliation, a step toward the Full-Hearted Community. And yet, there's a bracing message for us on a prominent grave marker still standing in the Colfax public cemetery. A large obelisk memorializes the three white "heroes" who "fell in the Colfax Riot fighting for White Supremacy." It reminds us that we're far from finished repairing the world. Research shows that, while Black Americans have made some economic gains, structural inequities persist in areas like the justice system, education, health, and civic engagement.[78] And the obelisk's message reminds us that, along with the imperative to dismantle unjust race-based social structures, we still have interior work to do. Work on the moral imaginary that created and justified—creates and justifies—the Colfax massacres of this world. Along with changes in our legal and political system, that interior work is how we become reconcilers right down to our marrow. The way of Jesus—the way of solidary and compassion—combines healing

---

76. See https://www.colfaxmemorial.org/.

77. Roberts, "150 Years After White Mob Slaughtered Blacks in Rural Louisiana, New Monument Tells True Story of Colfax Massacre."

78. See, for instance, "Annual Report Shows Systemic Racism Continues to Bring Down Black People's Quality of Life," *PBS News Hour*, April 12, 2022, https://www.pbs.org/newshour/nation/annual-report-shows-systemic-racism-continues-to-bring-down-black-peoples-quality-of-life; Ruqaiijah Yearby, Brietta Clark, and José F. Figueroa, "Structural Racism in Historic and Modern US Health Care Policy," Health Affairs 41, no. 2 (February 2022), https://www.healthaffairs.org/doi/10.1377/hlthaff.2021.01466.

of the soul and repair of our common life. Our work toward racial justice intersects and yet is not reducible to the work we need to do toward economic justice. So, let's turn to this issue next. A good place to start is with Alice.

## Economic Justice

Without Alice, the gears of our society would grind to a halt. You've probably seen her hard at work, but maybe you didn't take careful notice of her. Alice is our neighbor. She cares for our children and for our elderly. She waits tables, checks us out at the grocery store, and cleans our offices. Despite all her hard work and careful penny-pinching, Alice's bills often exceed her income. The combined cost of housing, health care, food, and transportation stretch her take-home pay beyond the breaking point.

Alice stands for Asset Limited, Income Constrained, Employed (ALICE). The United Way produces an ALICE Report outlining the financial insecurity levels for each state. In my own Louisiana, the report tells us that 32 percent of our households do not earn enough to cover basics. An additional 19 percent earned below the poverty level. In other words, 51 percent of all Louisiana households do not bring in enough income to keep a roof over their heads, food on the table, and medicine for themselves and their children.[79] The statistics vary from state to state, but we can find Alice in large numbers all across this country. And because I follow Jesus, I cannot see this reality as just Alice's problem. Alice is my neighbor. And Jesus taught me to love my neighbor as myself. So Alice and I face a common challenge: making a world where everybody has enough.

Before I go one step further, I want to acknowledge that some people might say that—given her education or ability or skills in

79. "Research Center: Louisiana," United for ALICE, https://www. unitedforalice.org/louisiana.

this economy—Alice is getting what she deserves. You may even have seen a bumper sticker on a car that reads "Nobody Owes You Anything." Well, that is one view of things, and it might be very difficult to persuade those who believe it otherwise. All I can say is that I can't square that bumper sticker with what Jesus teaches us, so I'm going to respond to Alice's situation in a different way. Jesus teaches us that we're in this complex, messy world together. My well-being cannot be divorced from hers. So I'll work with her to find a way for both of us to have enough.

Now Jesus was not an economist in the sense that we think of that profession today. But he had something profound, and startling, to say to us about the spiritual depths of our economic lives. God wants everyone to have enough. And deserving has nothing to do with it. Consider the parable of the laborers in the vineyard. A vineyard owner hires a group of workers at sunrise, promising them the usual daily wage: enough to live a decent life. He picks up another crew mid-morning, at noon, in the afternoon, and then just before quitting time. As the workday ends, the owner lines up the crews in reverse order of their hiring. Those who worked barely an hour, then those who came in the afternoon, then noon, and then mid-morning. Each group got the same thing: the usual daily wage, enough to live a decent life. Finally, the crew that had worked from sunup to sundown got to the payroll office. And they got the usual daily wage. They were furious. "We worked all day and got the same thing as those slackers who only worked a fraction of the time. They don't deserve that! We deserve more!" The owner in essence says, "Deserving has nothing to do with it. This is about my generosity. I have enough for everybody to have enough. So, I give it freely. Are you now dissatisfied with enough?" (Matthew 20:1-16, author's translation). The message is stunning, really. Enough will never be enough for me unless I want it for everybody else. In other words, working for justice involves a change of heart. The question that confronts all disciples is this: how do we go about the work of changing the world and changing hearts, especially when we will inevitably encounter serious resistance? To address that let's look at the example set by my friend Mack McCarter.

## How Followers of Jesus Work for Justice

Mack envisions a world where "every single child, no matter their age, can be safe and loved."[80] That vision led him in 1994 to leave traditional congregational ministry in Texas and to found Community Renewal International in his hometown of Shreveport, Louisiana. Two decades of church work had convinced him that cities and towns are essentially a web of relationships. When the relationships fray, those communities begin to decline. Crime, violence, addiction, child abuse, and high school dropout rates can be traced to the erosion of caring relationships. Community Renewal International works at restoring and repairing those relationships one neighborhood, one human heart at a time. One of the methods of Community Renewal is the Friendship House:

> A Friendship House is like a community center in a home, reaching out to at-risk youth and families with after-school programs, community service projects and activities that build positive relationships among family members and neighbors. A CRI community coordinator and their family live in the home and become an active member of the neighborhood.[81]

Crime has plummeted in each of the neighborhoods where Friendship Houses have been established. Community Renewal now has a presence in fifty states and forty-one foreign countries. But it was not an immediate success. There was resistance to the

80.  See "About Us," Community Renewal, https://community renewal.us/mack-mccarter/.

81.  See "Crime Plummets in Friendship House Areas," Community Renewal, https://communityrenewal.us/project/crime-plummets -in-friendship-house-areas/.

idea of healing the world's ills with something as simple and idealistic-sounding as God-inspired care for one another. For that matter, Mack still meets plenty of skepticism and criticism.

So I asked him once how he had kept going despite obstacles and in the face of opposition. He said, "I've had my last argument." In other words, there will always be people who are not willing or not ready to hear something new or different. They'll just be looking for ways to reject what you have to say. Save your energy and move on to people who are open to an honest conversation. It occurred to me that Jesus had something like this in mind when he sent his disciples out to spread the gospel in word and deed. He told them, "If anyone will not welcome you or listen to your words, shake off the dust from your feet as you leave that house or town" (Matthew 10:14). And we don't have to let a rejection like that get us down. Jesus is the one who sent us. We're doing our work, the work of reconciliation, on his behalf. When we make a friend, we're also making a friend for him. Here's how he put it: "Whoever welcomes you welcomes me" (Matthew 10:40).

Jesus's mission is to restore our relationship with God and to mend our relationships with one another. His aim was to heal this fractured world with the power of God's love. Taking up Jesus's work of reconciliation is what it means to be an authentic disciple. Jesus met opposition. And he was honest enough to tell us that we should expect nothing less ourselves if we genuinely follow him on the way of love. Sometimes we'll get weary and discouraged. But don't give up. Keep going. God is with us and working through us. And remember that Jesus tells us to use our energy wisely. Spend it on people who are ready to hear about doing a new thing; a loving thing. And maybe even come along with us. That's why I take Mack's advice. I've had my last argument. I'm going to just keep walking Jesus's way of love. And I'll walk with anybody who wants to walk that way with me.

# Spiritual Reflections and Exercises

1. Discuss what it would mean for you to be faithfully Christian and to uphold the ideal of the secular state. Does the secular approach to government express your faith? What challenges does the secular state present to you as a follower of Jesus?

2. It's easier to feel compassion for and solidarity with some people than with others. With whom do you easily experience empathy? How do you seek understanding and connection with those who are different from you and perhaps even in conflict with you?

3. More than half a century ago Martin Luther King Jr. said that Sunday at 11 o'clock is one of the most segregated hours in Christian America. In many places it still is. Talk about why you think this is so. What should congregations learn from this, and how should they respond to it?

4. Jesus set his followers on the path to reconciliation. What does reconciliation look like in response to historic racial injustice?

5. What do you believe about the source of poverty? What does Jesus teach his followers about their responsibility to the poor? Where does ministry to the poor, the unhoused, and the hungry fit into your spiritual life?

*Prayer*: Loving and merciful God, each of us is your beloved child. And yet again and again we fail to acknowledge one another as members of your holy family. Open the eyes of our heart to see the face of Jesus in one another. Give us a thirst for justice that will be quenched only by aligning our souls and our society with your vision of freedom, equality, dignity, and respect for all. In Jesus's name. Amen.

*It's good to do uncomfortable things.*
*It's weight training for life.*

—Anne Lamott,
*Plan B: Further Thoughts on Faith*

Epilogue

# Sweet Tea and Jesus

WEARING MY BISHOP'S PURPLE CLERICAL shirt, collar, and pectoral cross, I was ordering lunch at a Southern big-city restaurant with my friend S. No tables were available, so we sat at the bar. When our twenty-something server asked for our drink order, I asked for sweet tea. Tongue in cheek, I added, "I'm not sure Jesus will love you if you don't have sweet tea." Without missing a beat, she smiled warmly and said, "Well, I'm an atheist, so that really doesn't matter to me. But we do have sweet tea." I immediately liked this woman, more for her response than for the sweet tea. And she seemed to enjoy the brief exchanges with S. and me each time she stopped by to check in with us. If time had allowed for a serious conversation, I might have asked her about her beliefs.

If you've come along with me this far, you know that I've been saying that we all want to lead a full-hearted life. We human beings need to have a sense of identity: a sense of who we are and that we are worthy of love and respect. Authentic relationships are vital to a meaningful life, and we thrive best when we're passionate about some purpose. These are the elements of a joyful life. And all of these elements arise from our foundational beliefs. You see, our waitperson was no unbeliever. Everybody believes something. And that offers us a key to living in this secular world of ours. We will regularly encounter others who believe something other than our own Christian faith. Instead of perceiving those beliefs as a disrespectful challenge or a threat to our faith, we can recognize them as different. And difference is an opportunity to be curious, not judgmental or defensive.

Recall my conversation with my student Ellen, way back in chapter 1. Her family of origin had been thoroughly secular. She had grown up with no personal experience of religious traditions and no acquaintance with traditional spiritual practices. But you could see that she navigated her way through this world on the basis of a belief system. That belief system did not include God, but I'm convinced that it was in essence a faith—a non-religious faith, but a faith nonetheless. To draw on William James's definition of faith again, she believed in "an unseen order, and [that her] supreme good lies in harmoniously adjusting [herself to it]."[82] She had been shocked by the suggestion that I was, at least symbolically, a cannibal because I ate the body and blood of Christ. The idea violated her moral code. And since I taught philosophy and commended the importance of rational analysis to my students, she judged my attachment to an apparently irrational superstition to be hypocritical. From her perspective, hypocrisy counted as a serious sin, even if she wouldn't have used the word *sin* to describe it.

In other words, she had basic convictions about how we should treat one another and about what counts as a virtuous character. Her judgments rested upon a story she had about the grand scheme of things, about how reality works. That theory of reality leaves no room for the supernatural. Psychology, social science, and natural science tell us all we need to know about the human condition and how best to lead our lives. What I discovered is that she was not anti-religious. Her story of reality simply made no room for the

82. William James, *The Varieties of Religious Experience: A Study in Human Nature* (Oxford: Oxford University Press, 2012), 46.

supernatural and told her that religion was passé, an artifact from an era plagued by primitive thinking. Crucially, she had received her secular faith passively—from parents, friends, media, and teachers. She hadn't yet done the hard work of asking whether or not her faith story really held existential water—if it supported her distinctions between good and evil, provided a purpose in this life, or gave her an authentic sense of self. She hadn't asked, Does my story really work? For instance, how can someone insist on the equality of every human being when their perspective is limited entirely to the natural world? Individuals are clearly unequal in physical strength, eyesight, hearing, and intellectual ability. We Christians, by contrast, can say that everyone is equal because we believe that everyone is created in the image of God and that God loves each of us infinitely.

Here's how my faith urges me to approach the Ellens of the world and everybody else I meet. Remember that Jesus loves them. And so, I should too. An important expression of love is to take the time to listen to another person's faith story respectfully and to engage with it honestly on its own terms. In other words, does their story really work? That's what I did with Ellen throughout her college days. It's what I imagine would have been interesting to do with our busy atheist server that day. Additionally, once we've listened, we may have the opportunity to explain how the story of Jesus helps us to make sense of our life and to navigate its complexities. Or, as C. S. Lewis once put it, "I believe in Christianity as I believe that the sun has risen: not only because I see it, but because by it I see everything else."[83] In this way, we may be able to convey how Christianity could help them to make sense of their own lives. But remember, all of this begins by listening respectfully and actively.

The principle I try to follow is this: any friend of Jesus is a friend of mine. And Jesus has befriended everybody, whether they realize it or not. Now I admit that this is easier in some cases than others. A priest friend of mine once told me about a meth addict who

---

83. C. S. Lewis, *The Weight of Glory: And Other Addresses*, "Is Theology Poetry?" (New York: HarperCollins, 1976), 140.

violently disrupted a worship service she was leading. He stormed into the church, threatened her with a string of obscenities, and eventually slammed the door on his way back out. Her prayer in that moment has proved helpful to me a few times: "Well Jesus, you better show me what you love about this guy, because I'm really not seeing it right now."

Following Jesus means to navigate our way through life with the Spirit of love, because we know ourselves to be loved beyond reason. As the First Letter of John puts it, "We know love by this, that he laid down his life for us—and we ought to lay down our lives for the brothers and sisters" (1 John 3:16). Putting that in a slightly different way, following Christ means to walk the way of love, the way that Jesus embodied, exemplified, and inspires. The way of love is a way of intentional response to the risen Christ who walks along with us as the Good Shepherd, through thick and thin, in moments mundane and exhilarating. "The good shepherd lays down his life for the sheep. The hired hand, who is not the shepherd and does not own the sheep, sees the wolf coming and leaves the sheep and runs away" (John 10:11-12).

The Way of Jesus is a radical alternative in this world. We are God's beloved, and so is everyone and everything we encounter, however bruised and battered and disfigured by circumstances they may be. Each step we take can be response, response to the love we've been given as gift. Pure, unearned, unachieved, unconditional love: that is the essence of the full-hearted life. And to be clear, we do not achieve a full-hearted life by loving hard enough or loving just the right way. We participate in that life, the life that the risen Christ shares freely with us, when we open ourselves to his love and have the courage and the humility to pour that love out to the world.

# Acknowledgments

THIS IS MY THIRD BOOK WITH ABINGDON PRESS. I'm deeply grateful for their supportive companionship, creative input, and editorial guidance in each of these projects. Constance Stella played a huge role in making this book a reality. Months and months ago we struck up a conversation about themes in Christian leadership and discipleship. Initially my thoughts were disjointed and a bit vague. With the help of her insightful questions and gentle feedback, the connections between my seemingly far-flung ideas gradually coalesced into this book about the Christian life. I owe the phrase "full-hearted life" to her.

A number of my readers have journeyed with me since the early days of blogging, through the five books before this one, and now at my newsletter *The Woodlands*.[84] Their comments and emails have encouraged me, stretched me, and forced me to hone my craft as a writer. I give thanks for each and every one of my readers, known and unknown. And while I'm at it, I want to give credit to several of my bishop colleagues in the Episcopal Church. Michael Curry, Matt Gunter, Mariann Budde, Paula Clark, Rob Hirschfeld, and Nick

---

84. See jakeowensby.substack.com.

Knisely have taught me loads about following Jesus. And that's just to name a few. Authors like Lauren Winner, Diana Butler Bass, and Anne Lamott have shaped both my thinking and my technique as a writer. OK, I admit it, I've also envied their remarkable abilities.

My own faith life has been indelibly shaped by the people of the Diocese of Western Louisiana: their love for me and my love for them. I love the face of Jesus I see in them. And I'm humbled that they see the face of Jesus in me. By virtue of their grace and their encouragement I am able to be a bishop whose teaching ministry takes the form of writing. Among those ministering most closely with me are my staff: Holly Davis, Suzanne Wolfenbarger, Roy Rosenthal, Thomas Stodghill, Whit Stodghill, our treasurer Will Harp, and Joy Owensby (more about her in a moment). Along with serving as bishop of Western Louisiana, I'm also privileged to be the chancellor of Sewanee: The University of the South. What an inspiration that community of scholars, teachers, students, administrators, and staff have been and continue to be! The challenge of maintaining Episcopal identity in a twenty-first-century university inspired this book in no small part.

Last but not least, I come back to Joy Owensby: my wife, best friend, lover, and fellow maker of good trouble. Every thought and insight in this book bear her imprint. Anything good in these pages owes a debt of gratitude to her. The mistakes are mine alone.

Printed in the USA
CPSIA information can be obtained
at www.ICGtesting.com
LVHW012022181024
793924LV00002B/3